It's <u>My</u> Life Now

It's My Life Now

Starting over

after an abusive relationship

or domestic violence

MEG KENNEDY DUGAN, M.A.
New England College

ROGER R. HOCK, Ph.D.
Mendocino College

ROUTLEDGE

NEW YORK AND LONDON

Published in 2000 by
Routledge
29 West 35th Street
New York, New York 10001

Published in Great Britain by
Routledge
11 New Fetter Lane
London EC4P 4EE

10 9 8 7 6 5 4 3 2 1

Library of Congress Cataloging-in-Publication Data

Dugan, Meg Kennedy.
     It's my life now: starting over after an abusive relationship / by Meg
Kennedy Dugan & Roger R. Hock.
          p.   cm.
     Includes bibliographical references and index.
     ISBN 0–415–92358–1 (pb.: alk. paper)
     1. Abused women—Life skills guides. 2. Separation (Psychology) 3. Single
women—Life skills guides. I. Title. II Hock, Roger R., 1948–
HV6626.D84   2000
362.82'924 21—dc21
                                                        99-044898
                                                        CIP

Contents

For our loving, supportive,
and patient spouses,
David S. Dugan and Diane Perin Hock

This book is also dedicated
to survivors of relationship abuse
and domestic violence
who are, or will be,
on the path toward healing

Acknowledgments

Many thanks to Heidi A. Freund, Publishing Director at Routledge, Shea Settimi, Editorial Assistant, and Krister Swartz, Production Editor, for their commitment to and support of this project from the beginning. The authors also express their combined appreciation for the generous assistance of Timothy Russell, Chief of Police in Henniker, New Hampshire, and Michelle, a survivor of domestic violence, both of whom have been instrumental in educating their communities about the horrors and pain of relationship abuse and domestic violence.

Meg Dugan extends her personal appreciation to her husband, David S. Dugan, and mother, Helen C. Kennedy, without whom this book would not have been possible. She is also grateful to her New England College colleagues Muriel Schlosser, Dr. Joseph Petrick, Patricia Brown, Beth Varnum, and Michael T. McNerney. She would like to thank her sister, Elizabeth Delisi, her father, Theodore F. Kennedy, and her lifelong friend Virginia Page for lending their support through the many months of the writing process.

Roger Hock expresses his heartfelt thanks to Diane Perin Hock and Caroline Hock who lovingly and unselfishly endured the necessity of a *temporary* decrease in their treasured time together as a family during the writing and preparation of this book.

Introduction

This book is for women who have recently left an abusive relationship. It is a guide to help you through your transition to a new life, a life free of abuse, violence, and fear. This can be an exciting time for you; yet, as you know, it is also a period of readjustment, insecurity, anger, confusion, self-doubt, and, often, scary reentry into a new world. These feelings may emerge immediately after the relationship, or they may take months or years to surface.

Most books, articles, and other media about domestic violence focus on the abusive relationship itself: how to know if you are in one, why women stay in violent relationships, why you should leave, how to get out, and so on. Rarely is adequate consideration given to what many see as one of the most critical times for a survivor of an abusive relationship: the time after she leaves.

Not all abuse is caused by men in heterosexual relationships. Unfortunately, many women abuse men and same-gender abuse occurs in gay and lesbian relationships. However, abuse by men against women is the most common form of relationship violence. Consequently, this book is written for women who have been abused by men. This in no way negates the horror of abuse in other partnership configurations. Anyone who has suffered from relationship abuse and domestic violence will find the majority of this book relevant and helpful.

Those who have never experienced an abusive or violent relationship often believe that once she finds her way out, a victim's difficulties are solved: Her life is good, she is safe, and her recovery will be swift. But survivors know leaving is not the end of the nightmare. It is the beginning of a difficult, yet fulfilling and rewarding journey toward healing and happiness. This book can serve as your guide.

We have divided the book into three time frames that are relevant to the healing process for survivors of abuse: *Looking Back* (chapters 1 to 4), *Now* (chapters 5 to 11), and *Looking Forward* (chapters 12 to 17).

As you look back on your unhealthy relationship, your first step toward healing is acknowledging to yourself that you have, indeed, survived an abusive relationship. You may have no doubt whatever that you were in an abusive or violent relationship. On the other hand, you may be hesitant to define your relationship in those terms. Now that you are out, feelings may be surfacing telling you your relationship was much worse than "just difficult." Chapter 1 assists you in reviewing the characteristics and behaviors of abusive relationships. It will help clarify the nature of your relationship and help you move forward.

The next step in your journey is ensuring your safety. As survivors of violent relationships know, abusers can be just as dangerous or pose an even greater threat after the relationship ends. Chapter 2 offers some guidelines for maximizing your level of personal safety. This is a crucial component in your process of emotional healing.

If domestic violence is such an epidemic, why is more not being done to end it? Only recently has this form of abuse received widespread attention from the media. Chapter 3 examines many of society's expectations for men's and women's roles in life and relationships that have generated an unfortunate tolerance for relationship violence. Examining gender stereotypes may help you understand how these abusive practices could have existed and been overlooked for so long.

Chapter 4 addresses the "hidden horror" of sexual violence in abusive relationships. Healing from your relationship is even more difficult if it included sexual abuse. Many women may not recognize or acknowledge they have been sexually abused by their partners. Rape and other forms of sexual abuse are emotionally devastating experiences. If sexual abuse was part of the violence you experienced, you may feel an extra layer of pain and distress. You can get past this too, but some additional steps may be necessary.

Your current challenges begin with chapter 5's discussion of a confusing and often painful obstacle in your healing process: lingering feelings of love for your ex-partner. How is this possible? He's violent. He has abused you. Shouldn't this knowledge destroy any feelings of love or affection you may have once felt for him? Human emotions are not always "clean" and logical. In reality, many survivors of abusive and violent relationships continue to feel love for their partner after leaving. Discovering why you have these feelings and what they mean will empower you to move beyond them.

You may also notice you are experiencing a sense of loss and grief. These feelings are a normal part of losing any intimate relationship, even one that was painful and destructive. Relationships are complex, and, in some ways, violent ones are even more complex than healthy ones. Chapter 6 focuses on how the sense of loss you experience after an abusive relationship ends can, ironically, feel as distressing as losing a healthy relationship.

Now that you are out and in relative safety, you will begin to feel emotions that were not possible to feel when your main focus was survival. It is very common for survivors to experience intense anger, depression, and guilt after leaving an abusive relationship. Again, these feelings can be very uncomfortable and may be more difficult to work through than you expected. Nevertheless, they are a normal part of this painful transition. They are part of allowing yourself to feel again. Chapter 7 will guide you through emotions that may feel too strong and will help you regain those you have lost. Healthy emotional functioning is an important turning point on your path to recovery.

So, how much healing is left to do? What are some indicators that you still have work to do in your healing process? Chapter 8 will help you take a step back and consider some emotional and behavioral signposts along your path to healing. How are you feeling about yourself? How are you interacting with others? How are you functioning on a day-to-day and even hourly basis? What activities are you becoming involved in? Being attentive to these thoughts and actions can help reassure you that the healing process has begun.

Do you feel as if you are never going to get through this? Starting over after an abusive relationship is very difficult and extremely stressful. You may feel as though you cannot clear your mind long enough to focus on healing. You may be having difficulty sleeping or relaxing because the thoughts run nonstop through your mind. Chapter 9 offers suggestions for learning to cope with your stress. This will, in turn, help you deal better with life's daily activities, gain an inner sense of peace, and relate comfortably and effectively with those around you.

Sometimes other important people need to be considered at this point in your life. Chapter 10 focuses on the children who may have been part of your abusive relationship. Most likely, they were victims too, either directly as the recipients of abuse, or indirectly, as they observed the terrible events occurring in their home. Now they need protection from the violent ex-partner. You need to help them cope with what has happened. Dealing with the effects of the abuse in your children's lives can be complicated and emotional.

After you leave a violent relationship, you hope your friends, family, and coworkers can offer the support you so desperately need. Unfortunately, this is not always the case. Many people are so uncomfortable with the idea of relationship abuse that they retreat from it and from you. Others may not accept or understand what you have been through. Part of your healing process is deciding which people to allow into your life. In addition, you need to be prepared to deal with those who withdraw from you, disappoint you, or are unable to offer the support you thought you could count on. Chapter 11 explores the difficult process of dealing with the reactions of others in your life.

Although healing your psychological and emotional wounds is your chief concern, you may find many external, practical matters feel equally pressing as you begin to look toward a happier future. In the aftermath of an abusive relationship, many women must face difficult and often complex legal and financial challenges. These may include child custody and visitation arrangements, divorce proceedings, property and support disputes, and credit hassles, to name a few. Chapter 12 discusses the practical considerations you may be facing and offers guidance in finding the professional assistance you may need. Handling these issues effectively will help keep them from interfering with your healing.

What specific steps should you take toward emotional healing? Chapter 13 focuses on three of the most incapacitating emotions most domestic violence survivors face: anger, depression, and anxiety. It is important for you to recognize these feelings, assess the extent to which they may be affecting you, and take the appropriate steps to address them. You may find that you are perfectly capable of dealing with your intense emotions on your own. However, many survivors whose emotions begin to interfere with healing and moving on with their lives find that their healing process benefits greatly from the guidance of a trained professional counselor.

A major casualty of abuse is self-esteem. Many survivors judge themselves unworthy of love and respect. Rebuilding self-esteem begins with careful assessment of who you are now and who you want to become. Chapter 14 will assist you in examining your feelings and perceptions about yourself. As you begin to reestablish a positive self-concept, you will realize you deserve much more from a partner. You deserve to be treated with respect and kindness. It's not about finding a perfect, fairy-tale life. It is about knowing what you can and should expect from an intimate relationship and making sure that you get it.

For some survivors, one of the most confusing issues following an abusive relationship is the temptation to return to her abuser. He wants you to come back. He is saying all the right things about how he has changed, how sorry he is, how it will never happen again. He sounds so convincing! In fact, you may have left him in the past, only to return to watch the tension build and the violence begin again. Your friends and relatives are stunned, anxious, and disbelieving when you mention you are thinking of going back to him. You may be faced with making this crucial decision completely on your own. Chapter 15 examines the reasons you may be tempted at times to return to him. It also helps remind you of why you left. Making the right decision for you is a crucial step in regaining control over your life.

One of the most complicated and painful situations in the aftermath of an abusive relationship is that of a partner who is still in your life. If you had children together, you may have contacts with him, in person or indirectly through your children. If you live in the same community, you may run into him now and then in any number of circumstances. Chapter 16 will help you anticipate these contacts, maintain your safety, and protect you from further pain and abuse.

Can you ever love again? The answer is yes! However, a destructive relationship usually leaves the survivor with the very real fear of repeating the cycle. Healing from the abuse and moving on involve recognizing and avoiding potentially unhealthy relationships. Finding love again as a survivor of relationship abuse or domestic violence is the theme of the final chapter.

You are not alone. Many other women have survived the violence and regained their lives. Because abusive relationships are so terribly common, many sources of help and information are available to you as you travel along your difficult postrelationship path. The section at the end of the book called Resources offers books, Internet sites, and telephone hotlines to assist you in finding the support you may want and need.

Your new life may seem frightening, confusing, and overwhelming right now, but you are already well along the path to healing. It is possible to believe in yourself, have a healthy, intimate relationship, and be happy. Although the road may seem long and your destination is not quite in sight yet, it exists. It is just around the corner.

Caution: As you are reading this book, you may find an increase in intensity of certain symptoms resulting from your experience of abuse. Additionally, you may sense the appearance of new uncomfortable symptoms. If, as you read these chapters, you feel more depressed, anxious, or angry, or if you begin to question your control over your emotions, you may need to consider obtaining professional counseling to help you take full advantage of this book and begin to move forward in your life.

Note: The quotes at the beginning of each chapter represent actual statements from survivors of relationship abuse and domestic violence. However, the names have been changed and, in some cases, paraphrasing has been used to ensure confidentiality and protect the identities of the women concerned.

Meg Dugan
Roger Hock

Healing in Progress (I)

Where will you be in 5 years?

A helpful way to assess your perception of the future is to imagine in some detail where your life will be in 5 years. The following exercise will help you consider your goals and your belief in your ability to obtain them. Describe as much as you can about your life 5 years from now in each of the following categories.

Note: The time needed to heal varies from person to person. Many of the exercises in this book suggest that you repeat them in one month. However, you should feel free to extend that interval to six weeks, two months, or even six months if it better fits your personal pace of healing. It is also perfectly appropriate to repeat the exercises more than once if you wish.

Job or career _____

_____

_____

_____

_____

Intimate relationship _____

_____

_____

_____

_____

Family life _____

_____

_____

_____

_____

Friendships _____

_____

_____

_____

_____

_____

Physical Appearance _____

_____

_____

_____

_____

_____

Other _____

_____

_____

_____

_____

_____

Now that you have finished describing your perceived future, spend some time reviewing it. How does it make you feel? Do you feel happy and enthusiastic about the future you envision? If you do, that's great! You are on the right track. On the other hand, if you feel discouraged by your view of where your life is going, you need to work on starting over and healing from the abuse. This exercise is printed again on the following page. After 1 month has passed, try repeating the exercise. Comparing your answers will allow you to see changes and progress in your views about yourself and your life.

Healing in Progress (II): 1 month later

Where Will You Be in 5 Years?

Write down as much as you can for each of the following aspects of your future life.

Job or career _____

_____

_____

_____

_____

_____

_____

Intimate relationship _____

_____

_____

_____

_____

_____

Friendships _____

_____

_____

_____

_____

_____

Family Life _____

_____

_____

_____

Friendships _____

_____

_____

_____

Physical appearance _____

_____

_____

_____

Other _____

_____

_____

_____

OK, now compare your descriptions here with your responses on this exercise from a month ago. Are you more optimistic? More positive? More hopeful? These are excellent signs that you are healing and on the road to reclaiming the life you deserve.

On the other hand, do you seem to be even more discouraged now? Are you seeing your future as less promising than it looked a month ago? If so, it is a signal that you still have obstacles to overcome. We believe this book can help you move your life forward toward healing and happiness.

PART

I

Looking Back

1

Were You in an Abusive Relationship?

I'd heard a lot about abusive relationships, but I didn't think it applied to my situation. There were a lot of good times. I thought that meant the relationship couldn't have been that bad.

MARY, AGE 20

I never thought it would happen to me. I come from a good family, no abuse, and no neglect. My family and friends loved him. I figured the problem was me.

SHARON, AGE 32

Myth: A healthy relationship is one in which you never argue.

Myth: A relationship is only abusive if it involves physical violence.

Myth: Physical abuse is always the worst form of abuse.

Myth: If a woman doesn't get out of an abusive relationship right away, there must be something wrong with her.

*I*f a couple tells you they never disagree, never argue, never fight, you have to assume one of two things: One, they aren't being completely truthful with you or, two, there is something seriously wrong with their relationship. It is perfectly normal for two people who are intimately involved to argue. In all relationships, at one time or another, things have been said that are later regretted. Everyone has unintentionally caused emotional pain to the person they love. Because disagreements and occasional emotional pain are normal parts of healthy relationships, how can you tell if what you experienced was abuse?

Defining Abuse

There is no single definition of relationship abuse. Each intimate relationship is unique, and each abusive intimate relationship is unique too. However, as you look back on your relationship, you will discover certain signs, clues, and characteristics that will demonstrate clearly if it was unhealthy and abusive. Two of these signs are common to virtually all cases of relationship abuse.

First, relationship abuse usually involves a *pattern* of abusive events. Except in rare cases, a single incident usually does not constitute abuse. Instead, there is typically a pattern of repeated, destructive behaviors that escalate over time.

Second, abusive relationships involve the use of *power* and *control*. The abuser's goal is to ensure that he is in complete control of you and of the relationship. His controlling tactics may be subtle and not easily recognized. It may have seemed that his taking control of your time, friends, and daily activities was a sign of caring and of wanting only the best for you. As time went by, the control you once had over your life disappeared. Gradually, using a wide range of strategies, he was able to render you totally powerless and place himself in complete control of the relationship.

While all abusive relationships share these two characteristics, the specific behaviors used by abusers to achieve their goals vary greatly. At the beginning of your relationship, you may not have noticed the negative behaviors. Some of the behaviors may even have seemed loving and caring. His jealousy may have felt extreme, but he said it was due to how much he loved you. He constantly seemed to be around and told you that he couldn't stand to be without you.

As his behavior became more abusive, you may have grown a bit concerned, but you probably just dismissed it as a single event that would not be repeated. He apologized for his jealous outburst and *said* it would never happen again. He laughed about following you when you went out with your friends, saying he missed you so much he just had to be with you. Again, he *promised* that it would not happen again.

But slowly you began to realize that the abusive behavior was not going away; it was getting worse. Still, even as it increased, you may not have seen it as abusive. You may not have liked what he did to you, you may have felt hurt and unhappy, but you felt it was a normal part of a relationship, a problem that would be worked out somehow.

When you read about domestic violence and abuse in the media, it was always the most severe incidents that were reported. You saw the horrific stories of a woman who was murdered by her partner or a woman whose partner's violence sent her to the hospital weekly. You said to yourself, "No one deserves that!" These extreme (yet all too common) examples of abuse were easy for you to identify, but the abuse in your own life, while no less real, may have taken forms that were initially much less easy to see. In addition to the most obvious physical abuse, you may have experienced verbal, emotional, sexual, and spiritual abuse as well.

Physical Abuse

It seems hard to believe, but you may have experienced physical violence that you didn't label as abuse at the time. Not all *physical abuse* entails broken bones, bleeding, or stitches. Most relationship violence causes damage that others cannot see, so they don't even know it has occurred. Abusers become experts at it. Just think, if your friends, family, and coworkers could see the signs of your abuse on a daily or weekly basis, his (and your) secret would be out. Violent partners usually abuse in "silent" ways.

Your partner may have hit you hard enough to leave bruises, but he was careful to hit you only on parts of your body where others would not see them. He may have grabbed you and twisted your arm sufficiently to cause real pain, but he didn't leave a noticeable mark. If he threw you against a wall or pushed you to the floor, no one else would have known. Maybe he choked you so hard you were gasping for breath, but he didn't leave any marks that would allow others to suspect what was really going on.

Below is a partial list of behaviors that are examples of physical abuse:

- ◆ Pushing
- ◆ Hitting
- ◆ Choking
- ◆ Punching
- ◆ Cutting
- ◆ Destroying property
- ◆ Hurting or killing pets
- ◆ Shoving
- ◆ Grabbing
- ◆ Slapping
- ◆ Biting
- ◆ Pinching
- ◆ Hitting with objects
- ◆ Physically restraining (holding you down, pinning you against a wall, preventing you from moving or leaving, etc.)
- ◆ Physical intimidation (towering over you, blocking the exit, waving his fist, etc.)
- ◆ Rape and other sexual abuse (see chapter 4, "The Hidden Horror: Sexual Abuse")

Any of these behaviors would be considered physical abuse. While these behaviors may be easy for you to spot, some other forms of abuse are not so easy to see.

Verbal Abuse

Your partner may have abused you with words rather than, or in addition to, physical violence. Attacks of *verbal abuse* may have been directed at you or may have been in the form of negative comments about you to others. Your partner may have belittled and humiliated you in front of others or suggested to others that you were being unfaithful to him, even though this was not true.

Verbal abuse can be extremely painful and damaging and its effects long lasting. As with physical violence, verbal abuse can take many different forms, but the result is to change your view of yourself. Verbal abuse may have been designed to make you feel afraid and powerless. It may have focused on making you feel worthless and somehow to blame for what your partner was doing to you. It may also have been intended to convince you that you were small, unworthy, unattractive, stupid, insensitive, and so forth, and that no one but him would ever love you (see emotional abuse, below).

Here is a partial list of behaviors that are included in verbal abuse:

- Yelling
- Intimidating
- Name-calling
- Accusing
- Humiliating
- Belittling
- Using sarcasm
- Putting you down
- Rejecting your opinions

- Threatening
- Ridiculing
- Criticizing
- Insulting
- Blaming
- Mocking
- Treating you with scorn
- Disparaging your ideas
- Trivializing your desires

Of course, physical and verbal abuse take a terrible emotional toll. There is another category of abuse that focuses on your feelings and emotions themselves. This is referred to as *emotional abuse*.

Emotional Abuse

If you are like many women who have survived an abusive relationship, you may find that the physical and verbal abuse feels somehow less damaging in the long run than the emotional abuse you endured. Emotional abuse is so insidious and psychologically devastating that it can take the longest time to heal. Bruises, cuts, or broken bones mend faster than the wounds of emotional abuse.

There were probably many ways in which your partner was able to take control of and manipulate your feelings and emotions. Did he make you feel unworthy of love? He may have worked over time to convince you that you were stupid, ugly, or fat. Through these tactics, he persuaded you that no one would ever find someone like you attractive. By doing this, he was working to guarantee that you would stay with him.

Did he make you feel that the abuse was really all your fault? He probably tried to make you believe that there was something wrong with you because, otherwise, the abuse would stop. You came to believe that if you were only more patient, better organized, a better lover, or somehow different, the abuse would stop. But no matter what you did, the abuse continued. You slowly began to feel totally worthless and helpless.

After each incident of abuse, your partner probably tried to make it seem as though you caused it. It may have gone something like, "I'm so sorry *but* if only you hadn't . . ." He created a way to seem repentant while telling you it was really all your fault.

Did he threaten you if you didn't do exactly what he wanted? Threats can be a devastating form of emotional abuse. Sometimes an abuser's threats are overt and clear: "If you're late getting home, I'll break your arm." "If I see you talking to him again, I'll have to fix it so you'll never talk again." Other threats, though, can be more veiled and subtle: "Sure, go ahead and go out tonight, but I can't be responsible for what happens to your cat while you're gone."

Your abuser probably minimized the extent of the abuse in numerous ways. After he assaulted you he may have told you that it wasn't all that bad. This had the effect of making you feel as though you were exaggerating the incident. It also let you know that if this wasn't all that bad, much worse things were possible.

Here is a partial list of actions that constitute emotional abuse:

- ♦ Entitlement ("I have a right to sex." "I expect you to do what I say.")
- ♦ Withholding ("I don't need to tell you what I'm thinking or feeling." "Why would I want to make love with someone like you?")
- ♦ Emotionally misrepresenting ("You're not hurt—what a joke." "You're just being too sensitive.")
- ♦ Not taking care of himself (Doing drugs, engaging in high-risk behaviors such as driving recklessly, not seeking medical care, not bathing.)
- ♦ Withholding help (Financial, with chores, child care.)
- ♦ Excessive jealousy

♦ Threatening to injure or kill himself
♦ Threatening to hurt or kill you, your friends, relatives, or pets
♦ Controlling (Being in complete control of where you go, who you see, what you do, making all the decisions.)

Spiritual Abuse

Your partner may have found ways to exert control over you using something that is sacred to you: your spirituality, your personal values, and your philosophical beliefs. Did he ever try to use religious writings to convince you that his actions were OK? He may have quoted passages from your religion's sacred writings or your valued philosophical texts and interpreted them to imply that you were his property, that you were supposed to abide by his needs and submit to his authority and power, that if you disobeyed, you should be punished. No matter what spiritual convictions you hold precious, he may have attempted to minimize them, thereby minimizing you.

In addition to using your religious beliefs against you, your abuser may have denigrated nonreligious principles that are sacred to you. These beliefs are often an integral part of your upbringing and a solid part of who you are. Your convictions about your relationship to other people, to animals, or to the environment are a few of the beliefs that may have been fodder for his abuse.

Here are some examples of *spiritual abuse*:

♦ Trivializing your ideas, opinions, views, and desires
♦ Discrediting your values as unimportant, silly, or unrealistic
♦ Stating that his beliefs are the only "right" beliefs
♦ Using sacred texts to justify the abuse
♦ Using religion to justify his position as controller
♦ Denying your religious beliefs
♦ Preventing you from attending religious services or participating in sacred ceremonies
♦ Preventing you from observing holy days and rituals

♦ Ridiculing your religion and religious beliefs
♦ Intimidating you with religion ("If you don't do as I say, you'll go to hell.")
♦ Defiling or destroying books and other materials that represent your philosophical value system
♦ Denouncing or rejecting your cultural or ethnic heritage

A clear understanding of the many forms of relationship abuse and the specific behaviors involved should be helpful in removing all doubt that you were indeed in such a relationship. But beyond these behaviors is the bigger picture of the relationship itself and the process by which the abuse began, continued, and escalated over time.

The Cycle of Abuse

The process often referred to as the *cycle of abuse* (see figures on pages 12–13) can make it difficult for a woman to recognize that she is in an abusive relationship until the violence becomes extreme. This is because *no violent relationship is outwardly violent all the time.* Even if a relationship is violent on a frequent and ongoing basis, there are still periods when there is no overt violence. The violence and abuse typically follow a fairly predictable cycle. Another important factor in the cycle is that the abuse increases very gradually over time, making it difficult to recognize exactly where the abuse began.

If you were the victim of abuse in childhood or in an earlier relationship, the process of recognizing the abuse may have been a bit different. If all you had known in relationships was abuse, then you may have had difficulty recognizing that there was a problem. If your self-esteem and expectations for relationships had been damaged going into the abusive relationship, it may have taken a very long time to realize that this was abuse, it was wrong, and you deserved better.

The term cycle of abuse does not mean that once you are in it there is no way out. The cycle describes how an abusive relationship usually develops, unless something is done to intervene. Remember the beginning of your relationship? Everything probably seemed just great. He was loyal, devoted, and caring and seemed to have eyes only for you. It felt as if you had nothing to worry about. It was like a dream come true! If you had never been abused before, it may never have crossed your mind that there was reason for concern. If you had previously been abused, you may have begun to hope that this time it would be better, even if you didn't realize what constituted a healthy relationship.

However, after a while, something happened, as it does in all relationships, that created tension between you and your partner. It may have been a simple difference of opinion, a disagreement over a purchase or an activity, or just an argument about a controversial subject. Whatever the issue, it didn't seem like a big deal, but it disrupted the harmony in your new relationship. You expected that the problem would be resolved by talking about it, by working it out between the two of you. However, that didn't happen and the tension persisted. The only way you were able to regain the harmony was to give in to his position. You probably felt unheard and discounted by him, but it was really no big deal and if giving in ended the discord, it was worth it. So, after you discovered how, at least on the surface, to make the problem go away, the loving, harmonious atmosphere returned. The "honeymoon" phase of the cycle was beginning again.

But it was only the beginning. After a while another event occurred that once again created tension between you. This is called the "tension building" phase of the cycle. The same thing happened again, only this time there was an explosion: He yelled at you, ridiculed you, threatened you, insulted you, or carried out some other abusive acts. You were afraid and you did whatever you had to do to calm things down. And then, again, for days, weeks, and even months, things were good again and the honeymoon returned.

As time passed, this cycle continued, and each time the explosion was worse. The tension always ended in abuse. What began as insults and threats became physical violence. But always after the violence, the honeymoon began again. He was sorry; he apologized; he promised it would never happen again; he asked forgiveness; he was repentant; he bought you flowers and gifts. You felt the need to make things better and would do everything humanly possible to make him happy. Things would settle down although you began to feel that even in these good times you were always walking on eggshells. Compared with the other phases of the cycle, this felt like another honeymoon, and you hoped it would last.

The healthy relationship

HONEYMOON

PROBLEM SOLVING   TENSION BUILDING

The cycle of abuse

HONEYMOON

EXPLOSION   TENSION BUILDING
(ABUSE, VIOLENCE)

An alternative way to think of the cycle is to visualize a roller coaster. There were the highs when you felt on top of the world and lows when you couldn't see a way out. Each time you started that long free fall toward the explosion, you never knew what frightening occurrences would be next. After the explosion, the terrible ride would begin again.

The roller coaster of abuse

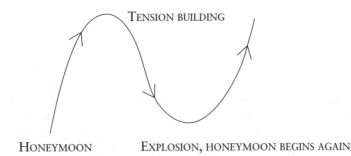

TENSION BUILDING

HONEYMOON   EXPLOSION, HONEYMOON BEGINS AGAIN

How Could I Have Been So Attached to Him?

People have probably asked you, "Why didn't you just leave?" Those who have never been in an abusive relationship often find it very difficult to understand how hard it is to escape even after the decision has been made to leave. Like many women, you may have asked yourself how it was possible for you to have become so strongly attached to your abuser despite the abuse you suffered. If this was not your first serious relationship, you may feel that, paradoxically, this attachment was somehow stronger and more difficult to break than previous nonabusive relationships. How could this be?

Traumatic Bonding

Traumatic bonding is a theory that tries to explain why abusive relationships are so powerful. Several factors have been identified that must be present for such a bond to form. First, for traumatic bonding to take place a relationship must contain an *imbalance of power*. Power has different meanings to different people, but generally it means that one partner is much more in control of key aspects of the relationship. If your partner made all or most of the decisions, controlled the finances, set himself up as the only authority, intimidated you through threats or violence, or made you feel powerless in other ways, the power in your relationship was completely lopsided.

The second factor in traumatic bonding is the *sporadic nature of the abusive behavior* as was discussed earlier relative to the cycle of abuse. In most abusive relationships, the bad times are intermingled with the good times. The abuse is usually preceded and followed by very loving, giving periods. This pattern of on-again, off-again abuse and affection is the strongest form of reinforcement.

The third factor in traumatic bonding involves a kind of *denial*. You were in denial when you told yourself, "It isn't really that bad." You devised excuses to make the situation seem somehow better than it actually was. You may even have altered your attitudes about the violence or found new ways of thinking that concealed the truth from yourself.

Even beyond this, if the abuse was very severe, you may have found ways of escaping the violence as it happened by imagining you were outside of your body, looking down on the terrible scene that was occurring. This psychological defense, called *dissociation*, can be a powerful tool to create distance between yourself and the violence. This is discussed further in chapter 8, "Signs of Unfinished Healing."

All these forms of denial and distancing are forms of what psychologists call *cognitive dissonance*. What was happening was so bad and so far outside any of your expectations about the world that it just did not fit into your sense of reality. So you relied on these techniques to try to make it fit. In order to survive, you had to change how you saw reality.

The last factor in traumatic bonding involves finding ways to *mask the abuse*. You may not have admitted the abuse to anyone, including yourself. Or, as often happens, you may have escaped from it through alcohol or other drugs. Drinking or using other drugs may have been a way of self-medicating. While you were self-medicated, it was easier not to deal with what was being done to you. It might have also been a way to deny that the problem was abuse and blame abusive behavior on drug use.

These four elements—unequal power, intermittent abuse, cognitive dissonance, and masking techniques—combine to create a traumatic bond with an abuser. Once this bond is established, it becomes terribly difficult to break free of the relationship.

The Stockholm Syndrome

The *Stockholm syndrome* is a theory about how a person who is being victimized can develop a bond with an aggressor. The theory grew out of a case in Sweden in 1973 in which bank robbers had held a woman hostage along with three others for 6 days. When she was finally released, it was discovered that she had developed a strong attachment to one of her captors.

The Stockholm syndrome also assumes four conditions exist that are similar but not identical to traumatic bonding. One, the victim is threatened with death or great physical harm and perceives the perpetrator capable of acting on these threats. Two, the victim sees no means of escape and, therefore, perceives that her life depends on her captor. Three, the victim feels isolated and holds little hope of outside intervention by family or friends. Four, the victimizer offers kindness along with the violence and thus increases the victim's perception of complete helplessness and dependence on him.

This syndrome has, in the decades since the original case, been applied to many victim-victimizer situations. It applies painfully well to abusive relationships where most, if not all, of these conditions often exist. When the syndrome emerges in such relationships, the victim clings to her abuser because he becomes her only hope of survival. This bond, however unhealthy, can sometimes be stronger than a bond that grows out of love in a healthy relationship.

Conclusion

An understanding of the behaviors that constitute abuse, as well as the cycle of abuse, traumatic bonding, and the Stockholm syndrome, should make it clearer to you how you ended up in an abusive relationship. It should also shed light on why it was so difficult to leave and why you stayed as long as you did.

Abusive Behaviors Inventory

If you are still wondering if your relationship was abusive, try taking the following quiz. Beside each behavior that applied to your partner, put a checkmark.

Check each of the following that happened on a recurring basis:

____ Yells

____ Does all the daily planning

____ Calls you names

____ Controls all the finances

____ Criticizes

____ Unfairly blames you

____ Checks up on you

____ Puts you down

____ Shows up unexpectedly

____ Doesn't pay attention to you

____ Doesn't give any emotional support

____ Always keeps track of where you are

Check each of the following that happened one or more times:

____ Threatens

____ Tells you who you can and cannot see

____ Isolates you from your family

____ Says he is always right

____ Towers over you

____ Threatens you with violence

____ Slaps you

____ Follows you around

____ Grabs you

____ Kicks you

____ Restrains you

____ Chokes you

____ Pushes you

____ Forces sex

If you find that you checked any of these behaviors, you may have been in an abusive relationship. Not all relationships are equally abusive but all are very painful and destructive in their own way. Although some behaviors are clearly more abusive than others, generally the more checks, the more abusive the relationship.

2

Are You Out of Danger Now?

He said if I left he would kill me. He always did exactly what he said he would do, so why should I doubt that he'll kill me?

DIANE, AGE 27

He never hit me or threatened to kill me so I thought I was safe.

CARMELA, AGE 62

Myth: Once you are out of the relationship, you are out of danger.

Myth: There is nothing you can do to increase your safety.

Myth: If there was no physical violence while you were in your relationship, there won't be any after it's over.

Note: Unfortunately, the risk of violence from a former abuser is all too real. You should never underestimate what he might do. You have the most insight to determine to what degree, if any, you are in danger from your former partner. You know your abuser better than anyone else. However, if you find that others (your therapist, crisis center worker, family, or friends) are telling you that they are more fearful for your safety than you are, be sure to take that into account. It may be that you are not fully ready to acknowledge the true risk that your former partner poses.

If you, or others who understand your situation, feel that you are still in danger, the following is provided to assist you in increasing your safety. The guidelines contained in this chapter should not be interpreted as providing complete safety from violence for every woman in every situation. Unfortunately, there is no way to guarantee your safety, but you should do whatever you feel is necessary to ensure your security. Take the time to read this chapter and try to judge how at risk you are. Remember, *never* underestimate your abuser, and never let others minimize your perception of risk.

♦ "Seventy-five percent of domestic assaults reported to law enforcement agencies were inflicted *after* separation of the couples" (U.S. Department of Justice).

♦ "Nearly three-quarters of the battered women seeking emergency medical services sustained injuries *after* leaving the batterer" (National Coalition Against Domestic Violence).

♦ "Almost one-quarter of the women killed by their male partners in one study in Philadelphia and Chicago were separated or divorced from the men who killed them" (The Domestic Violence Project, http://comnet. org/dvp/index.html).

These statistics are very frightening. But as frightening as they are, you know it was more dangerous to your physical and emotional well-being to stay in that relationship rather than to leave it. As you read this chapter and plan for your safety, you must keep reminding yourself that you made the right and smart decision to leave. It took a lot of courage and inner strength.

What Is Your Risk Level?

Now that you're out, what risk is there? Sometimes, once a woman is out of a bad relationship, the emotional relief she experiences is so great that she feels there isn't a need to be concerned about her ongoing safety. In comparison to life with him, she feels safe. But as you may well know, once you get out of an abusive relationship, concerns about safety do not always end; in fact, they may escalate.

You may still be connected in a variety of ways to your abuser through your children or other family members, or simply because you still live in the same community. However, even if you have broken all these connections, you may still be at risk. For many abused women, the *most* dangerous time is when they leave their partner.

If you experienced a great deal of violence in your relationship, ongoing concern for your personal safety makes sense. However, if your relationship involved controlling behaviors or verbal or emotional abuse without physical violence, you may think that safety is not an issue for you. Regrettably, for some women, the level of abuse increases after the separation, even if there has been no physical violence before.

Whether you recently left your abuser or have been out for some time, there may be a continuing danger from your former partner. Your abuser may not get on with his life as soon as you had hoped. Often, abusers plan and carry out violence long after their partners leave.

If you left your abuser against his wishes (which is usually the case), he is probably very angry that he can no longer control you. His abuse was always about control, and now he may be more desperate than ever to regain that control. His rage may be beyond what you have witnessed before because now he has no hold over you. This is often when an abuser carries out the worst of his violence.

How can you tell how much risk your former partner poses? It would be great if there were a perfectly reliable predictor of violence after an abusive relationship has ended, but there isn't. The best you can do is look for clues that the possibility of violence directed at you or your children still exists.

His Behavioral History

Perhaps the most obvious predictor of future violence is a history of violence toward you. Greater and more frequent past violence often predicts an increased likelihood of future violence.

Did he tell you that if you ever left him he would make sure you were never with anyone else? Did your abuser threaten to kill you? Threats of violence and death are good indicators that you need to be concerned about your safety. If he followed through on any of his threats of violence in the past, then you have every reason to believe he might follow through now that you have left him.

Another indicator of increased risk of being hurt or killed by your former partner is his accessibility to weapons. Does he own a gun or guns? Does he feel comfortable using a gun? Has he used the gun on you before, in any way? Has he threatened you with a gun before? All these factors increase the risks to you.

Was your abuser increasingly violent toward you? Over the months or years that you were together, did his physical abuse intensify? Did you have the feeling that it was going to continue to escalate if you didn't leave? If so, now that you have separated from him, his violence may increase even faster.

Think back to references your abuser made about the prospect of your leaving him. Were there veiled threats, such as "You know you really wouldn't want to do that," said in that tone of voice you knew meant violence? Did he directly or indirectly threaten to hurt anyone else that you care about, including your children, family members, or a potential future partner? Did he threaten to destroy your valued belongings or kill your pets if you ever tried to leave? If so, you would be wise to take those threats seriously.

His Psychological History

Something you will need to take into consideration is your ex-partner's psychological history. Is he very impulsive? Does he act with little or no forethought? During your relationship, did he frequently act on a thought or emotion without considering the consequences? People who are impulsive can also be very unpredictable. If his impulsiveness was part of the abuse, then the possibility of future violence is increased.

Did he exhibit rapid or extreme mood changes that led to violence? Was he likely to "fly off the handle" with very little provocation? Was he calm one minute and furious the next? Or perhaps he would seem OK one minute and then suddenly very depressed. Many people have fluctuating moods that do not predict violence. The danger lies in your former partner's sudden mood swings combined with his violence. If his moods were unpredictable and frightening, there is every reason to believe that this volatility will continue, increasing your risk of future abuse.

Does he have a history of depression? Do you remember that he went through periods of overwhelming sadness and feelings of worthlessness? Obviously, depression is not a sign of violence. However, depression, when combined with a history of controlling and abusive behavior, can increase the risk of future violence. Someone who is actively suicidal may feel that what happens to him doesn't matter because he is going to die soon anyway. If he feels that he has nothing to lose by hurting or killing you, it will make it easier for him to come after you (this will be discussed in more detail in the next section).

While it may be true that men who were abused as children or who witnessed the abuse of their mothers may be more likely to become abusers themselves, this should never be used as an excuse for their behavior. Having endured such abuse may have affected them psychologically, but the choice to act negatively on those emotions was all theirs. Having survived abuse does not give them the right to abuse others, although they will frequently use this as an excuse. If he told you that he was abused and therefore abused you, it's important to remind yourself that he still *chose* to abuse you rather than seeking help to change his behavior.

Another area of concern is your former partner's history of alcohol or other drug abuse. As you well know, when your partner was doing alcohol or other drugs, his abuse may have been more frequent and severe. It is important for you to remember that alcohol or other drug use does not *cause* abuse. However, drug use can reduce the abuser's inhibitions against violence and give him a convenient excuse for his violence. If your former partner abused drugs, your risk is greater.

His Mind-Set

What does your partner feel he has to lose if he hurts you now? The less he feels he will lose, the greater the risk to you. If he feels that his life and his freedom (from prison) are not worth risking on violence toward you, then the danger might be slightly less.

Whether or not he feels he will lose by hurting you is a very complicated question. Most likely, there are many factors influencing how he is weighing his potential losses. If he has expressed to you that his life isn't worth living without you, he may feel he has nothing at all to lose by hurting you. If he feels that he could not live with the "shame" (as *he sees it*) of your leaving, he might let this overpower any risk to him.

Did your abuser treat you as property? Did he act as though he owned you? Many abusers objectify their partners and turn them into things that are theirs and theirs alone. They do not see their partners as equal human beings. If your abuser saw you this way, he may feel that what "rightfully" belongs to him is gone and he has every right to do whatever is necessary to get you back or destroy you so no one else can ever have you. He may even try to damage you physically (such as by scarring or maiming you in some way) so that (in his mind) no one else will want you. If you were merely an object to him, the likelihood of violence toward you now is increased.

What about when your abuser says that he has changed? Perhaps he even tells you that he has been in counseling and is a completely different man. Changing abusive behavior and thought patterns is not easy. If you are considering letting your former abuser back into your life to any degree, be sure to read chapter 15, "The Temptation to Go Back."

All these emotional, psychological, and behavioral patterns, when combined with controlling and abusive behavior, indicate that there's an increased risk of violence against you now. The exercise at the end of this chapter will help you assess your current level of risk.

Reducing Your Risk of Violence

Now that you've looked at various factors that may indicate an increased possibility of present or future violence, what can you do to decrease your risk? The first thing you will need to do is assess your present level of safety.

Make an Escape Plan

If your abuser confronts you, it is imperative to know what you are going to do *before* it happens. In an emergency, seconds count. If your abuser shows up in the middle of the night and starts kicking in your door, you need to have an escape plan in place. You will lose precious seconds or minutes if you have to evaluate what is happening before taking action. If you have made a mental plan of what you would do in this situation, you will most likely react quickly and instinctively to follow it.

What are you going to do if your abuser enters your home? Think through how you can escape if he comes in by the front door or back door or through a window. If you live in an apartment building, be sure you know the various means of escape such as the elevator, stairs, and all the outside exits. Try to get into the habit of always leaving your "essentials" in a location that you can access easily and quickly. These essentials include your car keys, some money, a restraining order (if applicable—see the next section), and any medications you take on a regular basis. Make sure you know the fastest route to the local police station. If possible, get a cellular phone for your car and keep it with you whenever you are not near a phone. Be sure to learn how to dial for help in case of an emergency.

Do not share your plan with anyone except others living with you or those you know you can trust who understand your situation, and who might be able to help you with your plan, such as your therapist, a crisis center worker, or your local police. Think about everywhere you go on a daily or weekly basis and have a plan ready for how you would escape if your abuser appeared. This allows you to be one step ahead of him.

Create a Safety Network

Include trusted others in your safety network. Make sure that you have easy access to a phone in all parts of your home and that you always have a list of important phone numbers right next to it.

These numbers should include the police, fire department, and neighbors or close friends whom you can count on to help you and to whose homes you could go. You may want to request an unlisted phone number and give it only to those who understand your situation.

Try to enlist the help of at least two neighbors (you need to have an alternative in case one of the neighbors is not at home). Explain your situation to them, give them a complete description, and show them a picture of your abuser. Create a signal or password that indicates the need to call the police.

Tell the neighbors or landlord/landlady what you want them to do if they see him enter your house. Make sure they know that if they see or hear anything suspicious, they should call the police immediately. Be sure they are aware of your escape plans.

Be sure to inform the local police of your situation. Try to make an alliance with at least one officer. Having an internal advocate can give your concerns an even higher priority. Give the police a full description, a recent photo of your abuser, and any relevant forms, such as copies of restraining orders. Let them know that if you call them, they need to respond immediately. Keep the police department updated. If they are aware of the seriousness of the danger you face, they are more likely to respond quickly and effectively. Also, let the police know of any threats, no matter how veiled, that your former partner has made to you or any family member, friend, or companion. No matter how minor such a threat may seem to you, it could signal an increase in your risk of violence from him.

At times such as this, you may need to consider obtaining a *temporary restraining order* (TRO) against your former partner. This is a legal order that makes it a crime for him to threaten and harass you and your children. If he violates the order, he can be arrested. The exact nature of and procedures for obtaining a TRO vary by state. Your local police or crisis center can advise you about the exact process. Chapter 12, "Practical Considerations," provides additional information about restraining orders.

The Children

If you have children who are old enough to understand, include them in your safety plan. Be sure they know what to do and where to go if your former abuser gets into the house against your wishes. Teach them to go to a safe place in the event there's no one home. Plan for this ahead of time with your neighbors. Ensure that once the children are safely in another setting they know to call the police.

If your children are in day care or school or spend time with a baby-sitter, make sure those adult caretakers know the situation. *Be very clear about to whom your children may be released.* If possible, leave photos of your abuser with them so they will know if there is an immediate need to call the police. If your children are named in the restraining order, give copies to their school, day care center, and baby-sitters.

If you have pets, plan ahead for them as well. Have a leash or pet carrier ready in the event you need to leave quickly. Be sure the place you plan to go to will take your pets. If it will not, then find someone else who will care for them temporarily.

Take Charge

To ensure your safety you must become very assertive. Communicate clearly the boundaries you expect your ex-partner to observe. Do not allow your former abuser to talk you into something you don't really want to do, such as letting him into your house or meeting somewhere to talk. If he shows up at your house uninvited, call the police. Studies have shown that if an abuser is arrested, he is less likely to assault his partner in the future.

If you ever feel in danger, call the police. Some women are afraid to embarrass themselves by calling for help if it may not be required. Other women convince themselves they are exaggerating the danger and are overreacting. If you are not sure if the situation is going to be dangerous, always be willing to err on the side of caution. If you request help that turns out to be unnecessary, this at the very least alerts others to the possible danger. If you hesitate to call when help is needed, you could be making a mistake with dire consequences.

If you live in the same home you shared with your abuser, it is important that he know the rules and limits. If you have a restraining order, he has been told very clearly he *cannot* interact with you. There is no such thing as a minor violation of a restraining order. Any violation should be reported to the police immediately. If you have reason to believe you are in danger from him and have not obtained a restraining order, you may want to consider this option (see chapter 12, "Practical Considerations").

If you have moved to a new residence, you should not let your abuser know where it is. Be very careful to whom you give the address and phone number. If you are moving away and hoping he won't find you, carefully consider where he might logically look for you. If you are going to the town of a family member or close friend, won't he be more likely to look there? Wherever you go, you may want to get a post office box so your mail is not coming to your home.

Securing Your Home

It's a good idea to install a security system if you can afford one. They are available in a wide range of prices. Some include a "panic button" that allows you to trigger the alarm from various locations in the house. You should also make sure you have locks on all the accessible windows and doors. Make sure you have good outside lighting, and, if possible, install motion-sensitive lights. If you have any doors that are not very sturdy, replace them with steel or solid wood doors. Try to have some means of escape from all rooms in your house. It's a good idea to have locks on the inside of doors to various rooms in the house, particularly in your bedroom.

Away from Home

Unfortunately, your home is not the only place where you may be at risk. While it may be more likely your abuser will try to confront you at home, you may also be vulnerable to attack or intimidation at your place of work.

Make safety plans for your workplace as you did for your home. Inform security officers, receptionists, secretaries, and coworkers of your situation and give them a description and photo of your abuser. Plan how you could get out of your office quickly and be sure you have money and any needed medication with you. Keep an extra copy of the restraining order at work.

At work, make it clear to everyone they are not to give out any personal information about you to *anyone*. Remember, he could enlist the help of someone else to call and ask for your address or number.

If you have just left a violent relationship or if your ex-partner has recently been making threats, ask that someone escort you to and from your car. If there isn't a screening process to prevent unwanted visitors from entering your work area, talk with your supervisor about the possibility of moving you to a more secure, hidden workspace.

If you have any reason to believe your former partner may be following you, be sure to take various, alternating routes home. If possible, make sure you are never in an isolated area alone. Be alert. If you ever have the sense you are being followed, drive to the nearest police station. If this is not possible, then go to the nearest highly populated area. Do not go home. If your abuser has followed you, do something to get people's attention such as blowing the horn repeatedly. Lock your doors. Do not get out of your car. If your financial situation allows, invest in a cell phone. The ability to make an emergency call from the safety of your car can be a lifesaver. (**Note**: Dialing 911 from a cell phone may not work in some areas. Be sure you know exactly how to make emergency calls from your cell phone.)

If you think your abuser might find out where you live and come after you, another way to help protect yourself is to learn self-defense. Many police departments, women's centers, or colleges and universities offer self-defense classes. These classes will help you learn to defend yourself physically and emotionally. They can also help protect you from anyone who might attack you, not just your abuser. In addition, many survivors find that self-defense training helps them to feel greater self-confidence and gain an increased sense of control over their lives in general.

If you feel you need a weapon for protection, be sure to think this decision over very carefully. If you have children in your home, there is always a risk they will accidentally get hurt or killed by the weapon. You also must make sure you have thorough and in-depth training on the use of that weapon. Consult your local police department to see what they recommend in this regard.

Act Quickly

If, at any time, you believe there is an immediate risk from your former partner, do not hesitate to get help. This may include leaving your home and going to a safer place. Learn how to get into a local women's shelter. Explain your situation to the people at the shelter. Plan all of this *before* you actually need to go. Keep driving directions and necessary phone numbers in your car, at work, and in your immediate possession.

If He Finds You

Plan ahead for what you would do if your abuser confronts you. Think through all the possible scenarios, including home, work, and other public locations. Remember, the number one priority is your safety and that of your children. Think about what you can say or do to decrease your risk of harm. If the worst happens and you find yourself in a situation where your ex-partner is becoming violent and you cannot escape, do everything possible to incur the least amount of injury. Say whatever you need to say, do whatever you need to do to be safe. This isn't going "backward." This doesn't mean you're weak. This doesn't mean that you are returning to your old ways. It's simply finding a way out of an immediate, dangerous situation.

If he attacks you, make noise. Yelling something like "Fire!" is more likely to bring help than just screaming. If you are unable to escape or get to an exit, make yourself as small as possible. Get into a corner of a room or under some furniture. Try to cover your head with your arms. Be sure your neighbors understand that they need to call the police immediately if they hear any screams or other unusual sounds.

What All This Means to You Emotionally

Living your life constantly looking over your shoulder is physically and emotionally exhausting. When a real threat surrounds you every hour of every day, it tends to create unusual behaviors and emotions. You may find that you have a heightened startle reflex. When someone makes a loud noise or touches you innocently from behind, you may jump a mile and your heart may start racing. If you startle easily, especially when entering or exiting a room or place, this is not a totally negative reaction. It means that you are on your toes, alert to any possible danger. It's a very normal, biological, survival reaction. Your brain and body are working overtime to protect you. As uncomfortable as it may feel, you need to reassure yourself that it is OK to react this way for as long as you are living with this threat.

It is completely normal for you to experience nightmares. The nightmares may be about your abuser's finding and attacking you. The nightmares may be more vague: Something bad is happening to you that you can't control. These nightmares may disappear over the coming months or they may hang on for years. Do whatever you need to do to cope with the nightmares. If it helps to sleep with a light on, do it. If you feel more comfortable having friends sleep over, invite them. These are by no means signs of weakness; they are perfectly normal reactions to having survived a terrible ordeal.

Dealing with your safety is not easy. While you are taking all of the practical steps, don't forget to reward yourself for how far you've come. You decided to leave and you did it. You hope the day will come when you won't have to worry about being safe. For further discussion of how living under the constant reign of control and violence may have impacted you emotionally, see chapter 7, "When Feelings Overwhelm You."

In addition, if you feel this ever-present threat is taking too high an emotional toll, perhaps some professional counseling will help you deal with your feelings in healthy and effective ways (see chapter 13, "Beginning to Heal").

Assessing Your Risk

Below, you will find two copies of this exercise. On the first copy, check off each of the following that applies to your abuser and your current situation. A month from now, fill out the second copy and compare the two lists to see how your risk level is changing over time.

His Behavior

____ History of attempts to kill you*

____ History of threats to kill you*

____ Owns a gun or other weapon and has used it on you in some manner*

____ Increasing violence in relationship that included serious physical violence*

____ Increasing violence in relationship that did not include serious physical violence

____ Veiled threats ("You're really attached to that cat, aren't you?")

____ History of alcohol or other drug abuse

____ History of threats to kill himself

His Psychological History

____ Impulsive

____ Frequent mood swings that include violence

____ History of depression

His Mind-Set

____ Feels he has nothing to lose by hurting you

____ Has said he can't go on without you

____ Treated you like he owned you

____ Felt justified in his abusive actions toward you

Other Factors

____ Recent separation

____ He knows where you live

____ It is easy to break into your home

_____ No motion-sensitive lighting
_____ Coworkers are unaware of abuse
_____ He is allowed to enter your home
_____ He knows where you work
_____ No security system
_____ Neighbors are unaware of abuser
_____ Local police are unaware of abuser

*These factors by themselves indicate a high chance of violence in the future.

Assessing Your Risk: 1 month later

Now that it is 1 month later, repeat this exercise to see if your level of safety has changed. Once again, check off each of the following that applies to your abuser and your current situation.

His Behavior

____ History of attempts to kill you*

____ History of threats to kill you*

____ Owns a gun or other weapon and has used it on you in some manner*

____ Increasing violence in relationship that included serious physical violence*

____ Increasing violence in relationship that did not include serious physical violence

____ Veiled threats ("You're really attached to that cat, aren't you?")

____ History of alcohol or other drug abuse

____ History of threats to kill himself

His Psychological History

____ Impulsive

____ Frequent mood swings that include violence

____ History of depression

His Mind-Set

____ Feels he has nothing to lose by hurting you

____ Has said he can't go on without you

____ Treated you like he owned you

____ Felt justified in his abusive actions toward you

Other Factors

____ Recent separation

____ He knows where you live

____ It is easy to break into your home

____ No motion-sensitive lighting

____ Coworkers are unaware of abuse

_____ He is allowed to enter your home
_____ He knows where you work
_____ No security system
_____ Neighbors are unaware of abuser
_____ Local police are unaware of abuser

*These factors by themselves indicate a high chance of violence in the future.

When you are finished, compare this list with the list you made last month. If your level of safety has increased, that's great. Even though it may not be possible to create complete safety for yourself, you can be content that you are making the changes necessary to improve your level of safety.

If your level of safety has not improved or has decreased, be sure to reread the tips given in this chapter for increasing your level of safety. You may also want to talk with your local police department and domestic violence crisis center to get their recommendations for decreasing your risk.

3

How Could This Have Happened?

I *never imagined* I would be in an abusive relationship. I never thought it would happen in my town, in my neighborhood, much less in my home.

JOAN, AGE 55

I *remember a guy* in my high school who would hit his girlfriend. He didn't even try to hide it. We all knew it was wrong, but nobody really did anything about it.

MELA, AGE 19

Myth: Cultural stereotypes and beliefs have nothing to do with abuse.

Myth: Society's expectations for acceptable behavior of men and women are unrelated to their individual actions in relationships with each other.

How Society Facilitates Abuse

Culture plays a key role in creating an environment conducive to abusive relationships. You may have grown up learning and believing many stereotypes about men's and women's roles in intimate relationships. If you are like most people, these stereotypes exerted a strong influence on your expectations of yourself and others. Consequently, when you entered intimate relationships, you anticipated certain rules would apply. You may not agree with these preconceptions intellectually, but they provide a predictable, often comforting structure for complex relationships and, therefore, are difficult to dismiss. Unfortunately, these old myths often interfere with efforts to form loving, respectful partnerships.

The myths and stereotypes summarized here do not absolve your abuser of any of his responsibility for his actions. He had no right to do to you what he did. Also, this discussion of social expectations is not intended in any way to place responsibility on you for becoming involved or staying in the relationship. These insights into cultural influences are designed to shed some helpful light on why abusive and violent intimate relationships continue to exist.

Society and the "Myths" of Men and Women

How often do you see men rewarded for being shy, passive, or quiet? On the contrary, men receive the greatest rewards for behaviors that are assertive and, often, aggressive. The message that men are the ones in control is communicated at an early age.

You've heard the old expression "Boys will be boys." What does it mean to you? Usually it implies that boys are naturally more aggressive than girls. If a boy hits another boy, he is commended for "standing up for himself." You probably grew up in a society that not only accepts male aggressiveness, but endorses it. If a boy is not forceful, he is considered a "sissy." Boys who fail to stand up for themselves are often ridiculed and maligned. They are told that they will never amount to much if they can't protect themselves.

Moreover, boys are given the clear message that their job is to protect others who are "unable to protect themselves" (such as girls!). How many times have you seen, on TV or in your own life, a young boy expected to take care of his mother and sisters while his father is away? ("You're the man of the house now.") This seemingly innocent expectation sends a clear message. Although he is young, the boy is made to believe that the burden of protector is in his hands. He learns early to expect to be the one to assume control over others, especially females.

Equally influential cultural expectations exist for women. In general, women are seen as the opposite of men, not equal to them. Where men are seen as dominant, women are expected to be submissive. Where men are active, women should be passive. Where men are in control, women should be willing to obey.

"Men Are in Control, Women Obey"

Boys who grow up in households where the father is "king" learn the notion of male entitlement very early. If all household possessions are seen as belonging to the father, it sends the message that the man is in control of "his" house.

In a similar vein, boys raised in homes where the father is the primary disciplinarian learn that men are in charge of their own actions as well as the behavior of others. Boys see that others in the house need to do exactly what the "head of the household" demands or they will be punished. The message to boys becomes even stronger if the father has control over the mother too. Hearing the father tell the mother, "How could you have bought that without my permission?" or "I don't want you to go out tonight. I want you at home" models controlling behavior in unmistakable ways.

While the myths about men require they be assertive, just the opposite is true for women. There is an expectation that women will be demure and not assume control. In school settings, boys are praised for correct answers to questions and girls for neat penmanship. Boys are given implied permission to engage in active, independent activities away from the teacher, while girls are rewarded for staying close to the adult in the room and engaging in behaviors that are more dependent. Girls are expected to conform to rules for "proper" behavior. "Sit like a lady" and "Don't be such a tomboy" are just two expressions reflecting the polarization of expectations for boys and girls.

In families where the mother often defers to the father's wishes and demands, a clear message is sent that women are not in control. "Just wait until your father gets home . . ." is a common phrase that communicates to children that ultimate power lies with men. If your mother depended upon your father to dole out money, pay all the bills, and make all the financial decisions, you received another clear message about unequal power in relationships.

"Men Are Stronger Than Women"

Society expects men to be stronger than women. Projects involving physical labor are usually seen as the province of men. Even with children, chores are assigned according to the amount of physical labor required. Mowing, raking, and stacking wood are seen as boy's jobs; vacuuming, sweeping, and folding laundry are reserved for the girls. Girls are clearly physically capable of performing many of the chores designated for boys, and vice versa, but the culture determines to whom they are assigned.

Boys have traditionally been encouraged more than girls to participate in sports. Society sends the message that it is more "natural" for boys to be physical, competitive, and aggressive. They are expected to feel more comfortable using their bodies in powerful ways—ways that require strength and control to beat their competitors. On the court, field, or ice, boys are typically encouraged to be more aggressive than their female counterparts. When a boy is not aggressive in sports, he is told he is being weak and failing to perform up to standards.

"You throw like a girl!" "What are you, a bunch of girls?" These are among the worst insults that can be leveled at boys. The inference is that girls are weak and ineffective. These insults send unmistakable messages to girls that they are not as strong as boys.

"Men Are Served, Women Serve Them"

While boys are rewarded for their assertiveness and sometimes aggressiveness, girls, above all else, are reinforced for tending to the needs of others.

One of the roles most strongly instilled in girls at an early age is that of taking care of the people in their lives. Little girls are given baby dolls to "mother" and are rewarded for exhibiting nurturing, loving behaviors. The traditional female roles of cooking, cleaning, and doing dishes convey to little girls the clear message that they are caretakers. However, this does not imply that they should be powerful or in control. On the contrary, girls are often reinforced for *sacrificing* their own needs and desires in favor of ministering to the requirements of others. In addition, while girls are expected to intuit and even anticipate the needs and feelings of those around them, boys tend to be absolved of any responsibility for the emotions and needs of others.

"Men Don't Cry, Women Are Too Emotional"

Are boys encouraged to express sadness, fear, or anxiety? In general, our society gives boys permission for one emotion: anger. If a boy is hurt or upset, he may be comforted briefly, but then he is told to stop crying and "be a man." This message usually implies he should hide his feelings. Boys and men are supposed to be solid, unemotional rocks. Demonstrations of emotion are seen as "silly." Anger is seen as a sign of strength. Males are considered to be standing up for their rights if they react to a frustrating or undesirable event with anger. Outrage is often the only reaction to an injustice that is allowed from boys.

Boys are not only expected to avoid expressing emotions, but also supposed to avoid talking about them. Sometimes when a boy has experienced a sad or painful event, he will be unable to identify the emotion he is feeling. If and when he experiences sorrow, remorse, or other "unacceptable" emotions, he senses he should hide them. Consequently, he is left with no outlet for his feelings.

Throughout their lives, girls and women are given a confusing mixed message about emotional expression. On the one hand the culture expects them to be more emotional than men, but on the other it condemns them for being overly emotional. Women are often portrayed as purely emotional creatures who are so controlled by feelings that we can't trust their judgments. At the same time, childlike, silly expressions of emotion are often seen as attractive female characteristics. It is next to impossible for anyone to assume roles of power and control when seen as childlike and silly.

"Men Are Sexual Initiators, Women Passively 'Receive' Them"

Finally, what does society teach about the sexual roles of women and men? Sexual behavior is often a reflection of larger cultural beliefs. The message to boys about sex is that they are supposed to be in control, make "the first move," and take an active, never passive, role. Boys are also taught that their sexual needs are more urgent and important than those of girls.

Language is the mirror of a culture. Examining words and popular slang can often expose society's basic attitudes and beliefs. The words used to express sexuality offer insights into men and women and sex. Consider some common English slang for male and female sexual anatomy. Words such as "tool," "manhood," and "sword" to refer to the penis suggest power, strength, and even dangerous weapons. However, slang used for female anatomy creates a very different picture. Slang terminology for the vulva often includes terms that suggest something passive, a nonactive receptacle. "Hole," "tunnel," and "honey pot" are some common examples. More disturbing are colloquialisms describing female sexual anatomy as victimized by the male "weapon." "Gash," "slit," and "ax wound" are such terms.

The language offers further clues to cultural attitudes about sexual roles in its slang and vulgar terms for sexual intercourse. Words such as "screwing," "banging," and "nailing" (as in "he nailed her") suggest that intercourse is not a mutual, loving event but an act involving various degrees of aggression that the man perpetrates on the woman. This linguistic legacy demonstrates how culture expects different behaviors and attitudes from men than from women.

From an early age, girls are taught that it is the boy who should initiate romantic or intimate contact. The cultural expectation is that the boy should always call the girl, ask the girl out, or ask the girl to dance. Relationships are in the hands of boys. Girls are expected to be patient and wait. In addition, cultural tradition places a high value on virginity in women. But there is an implication that her virginity is, in many ways, under the control of men. After a woman has intercourse for the first time, it is said that her virginity is "lost" and the man "took" it from her. The inference is that she has no power to control her own sexuality.

Cultural Expectations and Abusive Relationships

How does all of this relate to your experience of an abusive relationship? As we stated earlier in this chapter, these cultural stereotypes and myths in no way excuse the behavior of your ex-partner. These deeply ingrained social expectations do, however, shed light on why abuse is so prevalent. They may also help to explain why it may have been so difficult for you to immediately recognize that your relationship was abusive. They also help explain why others in your life may have had such difficulty understanding and accepting your being abused. Examining society's messages to boys and girls may help empower you to reject these falsehoods in your personal life and in the society around you.

What You Heard Growing Up

Try to remember some of the myths you learned as you were growing up about men and women and their relationships. For each category below list all the male and female stereotypes you recall. This will help you to think about which of these myths may have influenced you and those around you.

Men are "assertive"_____

_____

_____

_____

_____

Women are "passive" _____

_____

_____

_____

_____

Men are "not emotional" _____

_____

_____

_____

_____

Women are "overly emotional" _____

_____

_____

_____

_____

Men are "in control" _____

_____

_____

_____

_____

Women are "caretakers" _____

_____

_____

_____

_____

Men are "sexual initiators" _____

_____

_____

_____

_____

Women are "passive sexual receivers" _____

_____

_____

_____

_____

4
The Hidden Horror: Sexual Abuse

My family knew about the black eye and the bruises. They knew how overly jealous he got. I just could never bring myself to tell them that he raped me.

ANDREA, AGE 25

I was so embarrassed about the rape. I somehow felt it was my fault. I should have been able to stop it.

BARBARA, AGE 56

Myth: If you are in an intimate relationship, it can't be rape.

Myth: It was sexual assault only if you kicked and screamed.

Myth: If it was your partner, it wasn't as bad as if it was a stranger.

*I*f you were in a controlling and abusive relationship, chances are you were also subjected to some form of sexual abuse. Many women who are in such relationships have a difficult time believing that they were sexually assaulted. Unfortunately, women are often raised to believe that an intimate relationship obligates them to consent to sex whenever their partner wants it.

It's important for you to understand that sexual assault is not about sex but, like all violence in an abusive relationship, it is about *power* and *control*. The sexual abuse did not happen because of his sexual desires or drives. It happened because it was one more way he could control you. He felt that he had the right to do with you whatever he wanted. He also believed that you had no rights at all, not to your feelings and not to your own body.

Were You Sexually Assaulted?

Rape is the forced or coerced penetration of any bodily opening using the genitals or other object manipulated by another person. Whether the penetration was vaginal, anal, or oral, it was still rape. You may have been forced into the act by violence, threats of violence, intimidation, or coercion.

If you were forced by your partner to have intercourse, you were raped. If you said "no" or otherwise clearly indicated you did not want to have sex and he proceeded anyway, you were raped. Just because you may not have screamed or yelled doesn't diminish the seriousness of what happened to you. Just because it was your partner or your husband doesn't mean that it wasn't sexual assault. No matter what your ex-partner may have said, you should *never* have to submit to unwanted sex with anyone. These acts were one more way your partner could make you do exactly what he wanted. Again, rape was a tool for his power and control.

In addition to rape, there are various forms of sexual abuse you may have experienced. If your partner touched any private part of your body—your genitals, breasts, or buttocks—against your will, that was sexual assault. Forcing you to dress or act in sexually provocative ways was a form of sexual abuse. If he forced you to be sexual with others, that, too, was sexual abuse.

All forms of sexual abuse are degrading and emotionally devastating. Because of numerous myths that exist about sexual assault, some women may not define what happened to them as abuse.

Sexual Abuse Myths

There are many myths about rape. One common belief is that men who rape have unusually strong sexual needs or drives. The truth is that sexual drive or desire does not cause rape and other sexual abuse. Rapists have not been found to have higher sex drives than nonrapists. It is also untrue that men always have a higher sex drive than women and, therefore, sex must be agreed to even if the woman does not desire it. If it was the case that your partner wanted sex more often than you did, this does not mean that his desires should have been given a higher priority than yours.

Another myth says that if a man becomes sexually aroused and does not have an orgasm, he will experience terrible pain or even be in medical danger (commonly known as the "blue balls" myth). This is simply not true. If a man becomes aroused and then does not have an orgasm, the blood that has flowed into his penis and created his erection will flow back out as he becomes unaroused. This process may be a bit uncomfortable (as it may be for women in the same situation), but it is never unbearably painful or medically dangerous; nothing turns blue or falls off.

A further myth about rape is that *stranger rape* is much more devastating than rape by someone you know. Not only is this not true, but it is often just the opposite. When you are raped by someone you know and who claims to love you, the trauma, fear, and horror are just as overwhelming as when someone is raped by a stranger. The shock may be even more profound because you never thought this person you chose to be with could be capable of such an act. The later effects are also sometimes more profound than in cases of stranger rape. Not only did you have to deal with the terror of what was done to you, but you also had to come to terms with the knowledge that someone you trusted, and once thought you loved, did this to you. If a stranger had assaulted you, it would be easier to say to yourself that he was a maniac, a perverted deviant, rather than someone you once loved.

How It Happened

Your former abuser may have tried to convince you that it was your duty to satisfy his sexual needs. He may have used religious beliefs (his or yours) to support this idea. You may have believed, and perhaps still do believe, that he had a right to force or coerce sex. Even if you do believe that, it does not reduce the pain and aftereffects of having sexual relations that you didn't want to have.

Did your abuser use sex as a way to make up immediately following an abusive incident? He may have said that it was the only way you could prove how much you loved each other. He also may have insisted that sex at that time would prove that everything was OK after the violence. You knew that if you refused, the abuse would start all over again.

The months or years of emotional and verbal abuse were setting the stage for the sexual abuse. Your abuser may have known that if he "wore you down" long enough, you would be more vulnerable to the sexual abuse. It's more difficult for all of us to emotionally and physically fight back when we don't feel good about ourselves, are depressed, scared, and isolated.

Another way your abuser may have forced you into sex was to threaten you with even greater physical violence if you didn't do exactly what he wanted. He always followed through on his threats before, so you had every reason to believe that he would follow through this time. Refusing his sexual demands was not worth the risk of increased physical violence.

He may have threatened to leave you or make life miserable for you if you didn't comply sexually. Enduring the sexual abuse may have been the only way you could escape even worse situations. If this was the case, remember: You shouldn't feel guilty. You did what you had to do to survive as best you could. You are not responsible for the sexual abuse. He alone is responsible for that.

If your partner grabbed or touched any private part of your body against your will, this probably made you feel demeaned and afraid. He may have engaged in his unacceptable touching in order to demonstrate his ownership of your body. When you aren't able to control what happens to your body, you are rendered powerless. This is exactly how your abuser was trying to make you feel.

You may have suffered the trauma of being forced into sexual acts against your will with people other than him. Not only were you unable to control what was done to your body, you were unable to control who did it. If this happened to you, it may have been even more humiliating and frightening and the fear of what else they might do to you was terrifying. You may have been constantly terrified of the possibility of getting pregnant or contracting HIV or other sexually transmitted diseases.

Your former partner may have forced you to have sex with others for money. He may have profited from your abasement and fear. If you were forced to do this, it is important to realize that in many ways you were being kept as a slave. You felt you had no way to escape these horrors. Again, you endured these humiliations to survive.

All of these forms of sexual assault make you feel embarrassed and ashamed even though *you did nothing wrong*. Your abuser made you do things you otherwise would never have done. They in no way reflect your true desires or who you really are.

The Effects of Sexual Assault

Even though the person who sexually assaulted you was your partner, you may have feared he might kill you. Even if there was no other violence before this, you still may have feared for your life. Sexual assault was so unthinkable, you probably couldn't imagine what he might do to you next.

If you had already experienced physical violence from your abuser, the fear of violence at the time of the sexual assault may have been greatly heightened. And after the sexual violence you probably felt that the threat of all kinds of violence from your partner was much greater.

Shock

If you are like many women, you may have gone through a state of shock after the sexual assault. Even if you had endured other forms of abuse from your former partner, the sexual assault may have seemed like something that would never happen. Many women say that during the actual sexual abuse episode and for days, weeks, or months after, they felt as though in a dream—a nightmare from which they couldn't awaken. What happened was so out of context with everything they believed about life and relationships, it didn't fit into reality.

You probably suffered from nightmares. The nightmares may have been reenactments of the assault, or maybe they depicted other terrifying occurrences that you were unable to escape. Your nightmares may have been exaggerated by your having to sleep in the same bed with the person who did this to you.

Self-Esteem

You may have had other reactions in the days following the abuse, such as feeling dirty and ashamed. You may have taken numerous showers or baths and still not felt clean. If you felt comfortable with your body before the assault, that may have changed. You may have begun to feel ashamed of your body and wanted to hide any hint of sexuality by wearing baggy clothes, neglecting your personal hygiene, and even changing your eating patterns.

It is possible that during one or more of the sexual assaults, your body responded to the physical stimulation. If you found that your body responded to the physical stimulation (your vagina became lubricated or you had an orgasm), this is not an indication that you "wanted" to be assaulted. It doesn't mean the assault wasn't so terrible. All that it means is that your body responded reflexively to direct physical stimulation.

If you felt there was no way out of the relationship, as most victims do, then you may have stayed with your partner for some time after the sexual abuse began. As with all the forms of abuse, the sexual abuse probably came and went. At times, your partner may have seemed very caring, understanding, and sensual rather than intimidating and frightening. If you resumed sexual relations with him, this is one more piece of evidence that points to how complicated and perplexing these relationships can be. It does not mean you are a bad person or that having sex with him voluntarily was wrong.

Trust

If your partner sexually assaulted you, you know firsthand the confusion and the complex mix of emotions you experienced. If your trust in your partner had not already been completely destroyed, it certainly was now. If you stayed in the relationship, you probably began to question what else he might do to you. If he could do something this hateful, were there no limits to his abuse?

Perhaps you started to question your ability to judge who is trustworthy and who is not. After all, you originally trusted this man and believed that he would never hurt you. In reality, you had no way of knowing that he was capable of doing such a thing, yet you may have spent a great deal of time beating yourself up for not seeing this coming. Just as with the other forms of abuse you endured from him, a sexual assault was totally unimaginable before it happened.

Sexual Feelings

The sexual abuse you endured may have ended any sexual desire you had for your abuser. After the first episode, you may have wanted never to be sexual with him again. This is a very normal reaction to such a horrible event. From then on, all sexual contact with him may have felt like another sexual assault.

As with the other forms of abuse, he may have convinced you that he was sorry and that it would never happen again. You wanted to believe him, and although the assault did great damage, you may not have blamed your partner at first. You tried to get past it and may even have returned to a consensual and desirous sexual life with him.

If during any part of the sexual abuse your body became sexually aroused, he may have tried to convince you that, therefore, you really wanted and liked it. You know that nothing could be further from the truth. Remember, physical responses to direct stimulation are sometimes possible regardless of your emotional and psychological reactions. Regardless of any arousal you may have experienced during the abuse, you did not like it or want it. No one does.

Anxiety and Vigilance

After you were assaulted, you may have found your overall level of anxiety greatly increased. Everyday events unrelated to the attack created unrealistic worry and concern. You may have felt increased anxiety in your body as well. You may have developed headaches, backaches, or stomachaches. Your neck may have felt frequently stiff and painful.

Did you find that you became more "jumpy" following the sexual assault? If you had already suffered physical abuse, you may have experienced this after those attacks as well. If there was a sudden loud noise, you may have felt you jumped a mile. If someone unexpectedly touched you from behind, you were extremely startled. You flinched, your heart raced, and you broke into a cold sweat. You may have felt as though you were always on alert, ready for something bad to happen. This reaction, known as *hypervigilance*, may have lasted for weeks, months, or years.

You may have experienced a psychological condition called *intrusive recall*. Intrusive recall means that suddenly, without warning, your mind became immersed in thoughts of the assault. This recall would, at times, happen out of the blue. It may have felt like a horrible daydream or it may have seemed more like a flashback. It was almost as if the assault were happening all over again. You may have reacted verbally or physically to such a flashback by yelling, crying, or curling up into a fetal position. Both of these reactions to trauma, hypervigilance, and intrusive recall are discussed further in chapter 8, "Signs of Unfinished Healing."

Depression

Perhaps the most common reaction to being sexually assaulted is depression. You probably got to the point where you felt an overwhelming sense of sadness and loss. He took something precious away from you: control over your body, your feelings, and your life. In a matter of minutes or hours, he took a huge part of you that will take a long time to regain. This depression was caused not only by the realization of all you lost but also by the knowledge that someone you had trusted and loved had violated you. If you were already depressed, this assault may have made it much worse.

While you were depressed your eating and sleeping patterns may have changed. Suddenly, you may have had difficulty falling or staying asleep. In every waking moment, you were so emotionally distraught by the sexual assault that it wasn't possible to sleep. On the other hand, you may have slept all the time, trying to escape any thought or memory of what had happened to you. Your depression may have caused similar changes in your eating patterns. Eating concerns will be discussed more in the Self-Destructive Behaviors section below.

Your depression may have been accompanied by fatigue. Everyday activities may have seemed overwhelming. Simple tasks like brushing your teeth or making a meal may have seemed insurmountable. You may have found yourself losing interest in activities you used to enjoy such as working out, listening to music, reading, or crafts.

As discussed earlier, your self-esteem may have been influenced by this sexual attack as much as or more than by the other types of abuse you may have suffered. If you felt OK about yourself prior to the sexual abuse, you may have found you hated yourself afterward. This loss of self-esteem probably stemmed not only from the depression but also from self-blame and anger. If your belief in yourself was shaky to begin with, the assault may have destroyed it completely.

One of your partner's goals was to ensure that you would stay with him. The sexual attack may have convinced you that you were unworthy of anyone else's love. Consequently, if you thought you didn't deserve to be treated better, it may have been even more difficult for you to leave the relationship. The sexual assault was one more way for him to keep you right where he wanted you.

If your depression became too intense, you may have become suicidal. Sexual assault combined with feeling trapped in the relationship may have made you decide life was not worth living. But you didn't kill yourself. That you are still here is an incredible testament to your inner strength.

Anger

Another normal reaction to rape is anger. Some women feel an overpowering rage that consumes every thought and feeling. But in your situation if you dared to display your anger, the situation would have become much worse. Instead of being able to vent your anger, you had to bottle it up inside.

You may have taken your anger out on those around you other than your abuser: your children, family, friends, or coworkers. This may have been the only way in which you could release some of that fury.

Or you may have taken the anger out on yourself. Maybe you started to blame yourself for getting into this horrible situation in the first place. You may even have started to hate yourself. This self-hatred may have caused you to seek other ways to hurt yourself.

Self-Destructive Behaviors

Increasing your alcohol or drug use may have been a way for you to deal with the anger and cope with the pain. You may have self-medicated to try to stay "sane."

You may have found eating was another means of escape. If the attacks made you want to bury your sexuality, you may have thought that by altering your body, you would become less sexually desirable. You thought that if you were less attractive, maybe the assaults would end.

Perhaps you found yourself eating much more than you had before in order to gain weight. In your mind you may have thought that being overweight would make you less sensual. Or you may have tried to do just the opposite. You may have reduced your eating and lost a lot of weight. You may have felt that by becoming very thin you would become less sexual, your chest would be flatter; you would have a more boylike figure. You may also have felt you had some control over at least one part of your life: your eating.

Self-injurious behaviors such as cutting yourself may have been another outlet for your anger and distress. If, after being raped, you felt nothing or felt anger toward yourself, cutting may have become a routine. If you cut yourself, perhaps it was to feel something at a time when you seemed completely numb. Cutting yourself may also have been an attempt to punish yourself for what you thought was somehow your fault.[1]

Denial

After the sexual assault, you may have tried to block the entire event from your conscious mind. You may have avoided thinking about it at all for quite some time. On the other hand, you may have remembered it, but your memory somehow altered it to be much less traumatic than it actually was. Only later, when you were out and safe, did something trigger your memory of the event and the full impact of what happened finally hit you. Perhaps days, weeks, or months later, the assault may suddenly have overwhelmed you.

If you did manage to push the horror of what happened aside for a while, it is very important you recognize why this happened. Unfortunately, many women blame themselves for not realizing sooner just how bad the sexual assault was. They worry that if they had realized it sooner, they could have left sooner. Usually, this is not the case. If you managed to suppress the trauma of what was happening, it was for a good reason. Feeling the full psychological force of the sexual abuse at the time it happened might have made you unable to go on. It would have made your life totally unbearable to feel there was no way out. You might have become deeply depressed and possibly suicidal. The denial probably helped to save you.

[1] For additional information on this topic, refer to Smith, G., Cox, D., & Saradjian, J. (1998). *Women and self-harm: Understanding, coping, and healing from self-mutilation.* New York: Routledge.

Isolation

The sexual assault may have caused you to become even more isolated than you were already. The guilt, embarrassment, depression, and decreased self-esteem made you avoid those who might have been able to help. Trying to hide or explain this part of the abuse may have been just too much for you.

Any one or a combination of these effects of sexual assault may have felt devastating to you. Trying to cope with the reality of it at the same time you were experiencing nightmares, jumping at every noise or touch, and reliving the incident in your mind over and over again may have made you feel as if you were truly going crazy. You were, of course, having a normal reaction to a horrible and terrifying trauma.

What Now?

Now that you are out of the abusive relationship, one of the things that you may find very difficult is coming to terms with your sexuality. If you were sexually assaulted, you may find that you now feel no sexual desire at all, for anyone. This is a common reaction after such abuse. The healing process can take a long time and involves not only healing your feelings of sexual desire but also healing your ability to trust another person.

Everyone is different and the effects suffered from sexual abuse vary. You may have experienced some or all of these reactions. There is no timetable for when you should be over these symptoms. Some effects come on quickly and last for weeks or months. Others may not begin until much later and last for a very long time.

If you were sexually assaulted, there will probably be events that trigger old reactions of fear, depression, anxiety, anger, or mistrust throughout your life. Over time, these reactions should become more bearable, but, most likely, they will never go away completely. You may not always know what it is that triggers these responses. It may be obvious events such as a movie in which a rape occurs, or it may be as subtle as walking by someone who wears the same cologne your abuser wore.

If you find yourself having a reaction, even if you don't know why, it's OK. There is no mental health milestone you have to pass at any certain time. You are *not* crazy for having these reactions, whether it's been a month, a year, or 5 years. They are perfectly normal.

It won't always be as bad as it might be right now for you. Survivors of rape and other forms of sexual abuse will talk about the pain slowly lifting. If the pain you feel is particularly acute or if you find that the pain is not getting better as time goes by, then you may want to get extra help and support.

You may find it helpful to read books and articles about healing from sexual abuse. (See "Resources" at the end of this book.) Finding a survivor's support group may also be helpful. Talking with other women who went through a similar experience can be very empowering. You may also want to talk with someone from a rape crisis center or a therapist who specializes in this area (see chapter 13, "Beginning to Heal"). Getting help does not mean you are weak. It means you are taking care of yourself.

Being sexually assaulted was not your fault. You did nothing to bring this on, and you in no way deserved it. Over time the feeling of numbness will fade as you regain the life you want. Also, as time goes on, you should be able to recognize with clarity and confidence that you do not deserve to be hurt ever again—not by anyone, including yourself.

Self-Talk

This exercise involves remembering what you've been through and what it took to survive. All the thoughts below are designed to help you feel better about yourself. Take time each day to read silently or aloud the items that you need to remember the most. Copy down these most relevant items and put them up in places around your house where you will see them on a daily basis: on the refrigerator, on a mirror, in your car, and so forth. These affirmations will remind you to respect and take good care of yourself.

+ *I know I was in no way responsible for the sexual assault.*

+ *I went through a very traumatic sexual assault, and it is normal to have severe reactions to it.*

+ *No matter what I was forced to do, I know it was caused by (abuser's name).*

+ *It's OK to have different emotions from someone who has never been sexually assaulted.*

+ *Just because (your abuser) was not the person I thought he was does not mean I am a poor judge of character.*

+ *I will try to stop scolding myself for things I can't change.*

+ *I am as good as anyone else and deserve to be treated as well as anyone else.*

+ *I deserve to be treated with respect, caring, and sensitivity.*

+ *I will treat myself with respect, caring, and sensitivity.*

+ *I am proud that I was able to survive his abuse.*

+ *I now know that I am a strong, intelligent, and courageous person.*

PART

II

Now

5

Do You Still Love Him?

He put me through hell. I can't believe that I could still have feelings for him. What's wrong with me?

TERRY, AGE 43

I can't talk to anyone about it. If I say the slightest positive thing about him, my family jumps all over me. In some ways, I'm as isolated as I was when I was still with him.

FRANCES, AGE 65

Myth: Once someone has abused you, all your love for him is gone.

Myth: Anyone who could love someone who abused her must have a psychological problem.

What Is Love?

It would be an easier world if love were always rational and predictable: You find the right person, you fall in love, you treat each other with respect, tenderness, and caring, and you live happily ever after. Unfortunately, love is not always rational. Love does not always live up to expectations. Love isn't even always based on how he treats you. No, love is a very rich, complex, and often puzzling set of emotions. People often fall in love without really knowing everything about their partner, without knowing for sure how they will be treated. And once you are in love, it can be very difficult to fall out of love.

When this is true in an abusive relationship, it can be extremely confusing. Many survivors feel hatred or nothing at all toward their abusers, but many others torture themselves with painful questions: "How could I still love him after what he did to me?" "He hurt me; he was cruel to me; so how can I still have these feelings for him?" "Doesn't this mean there is something wrong with me?" The answer to this last question is: "No!" These feelings and questions are common and perfectly normal.

It Was So Good at First

You know your relationship was abusive, even violent. You know it was fundamentally unhealthy. You know this now. But for most survivors the abusive relationships did not start out that way. On the contrary, things were wonderful at first: He was attentive, caring, and committed. You were drawn to him for many reasons. When you think back to the early days of the relationship, you can picture the gifts he gave you, how he wanted to be with you all the time, and how he told you he loved you more than anyone else ever could.

No one, not even your abuser, is all good or all bad. There were genuinely good characteristics that made you fall in love with him. His sense of humor, his ability to work on cars, his passion for reading, or his looks may be attributes that are part of who he was and is. Unfortunately, as time went on, you realized that all these positive qualities could not override the control and abuse.

Early in the relationship, he may have awakened in you brand-new emotions about yourself; maybe for the first time you felt you deserved to be treated well. You felt lucky to have found such a loving, devoted partner. At the beginning, it may have seemed that he was treating you better than anyone ever had. He was protective, generous in some ways, he complimented you a lot, he was even jealous. You may have seen his jealousy as a flattering sign of how much he cared for you. Thinking back, you can remember conversations between the two of you about special and rare qualities of your relationship.

If you came into this relationship with a history of childhood abuse or abuse in other intimate relationships, it is possible that it was even more difficult for you to immediately recognize the danger signs. Some women who have endured repeated abuse may fail to realize that they deserve or should expect anything better (see chapter 17, "Loving Again"). This by no means excuses the abuse or makes you somehow to blame. It simply may help you to let go of some of your guilt or confusion about not recognizing the abuse earlier.

Recognizing the Signs of Abuse

It is very painful to discover now that many of his "special" characteristics were actually signs of the abuse to come. His attentiveness, possessiveness, and jealousy that seemed so charming and endearing turned into control, abuse, and violence. With this discovery comes the feeling that you failed in some way. You didn't see it coming. So, now, you are questioning your own ability to find a healthy relationship.

Giving up your love for him may feel as though you are also abandoning your ability to love and be loved. It can take time after leaving an abusive relationship to understand that some of his qualities that attracted you initially were, in fact, not healthy ones. However, this does not mean that you are not capable of loving someone truly and deeply. It also does not imply that you are unworthy of being loved in return in the same way.

Why Couldn't You See the Change?

Another obstacle survivors face in moving past feelings of love for their abuser is identifying when the relationship went from good to bad. When did it change? Why wasn't there a specific point when you said, "That's it; I will no longer love this person"? If this question feels difficult or even impossible to answer, that's because it is. Usually, abuse creeps into a relationship in an insidious, gradual way, over months or years. There is rarely a precise moment or single event that defines the beginning of the abuse.

What else was happening in your relationship as the abuse was growing? Chances are your love, caring, and devotion for him were growing as well. The love came first and then kept pace with the abuse. To try to pinpoint the moment when the abuse outweighed the love may not be possible.

This is made more confusing by the fact that abusive relationships are not overtly abusive all the time. Many of the controlling behaviors were so well hidden they were barely recognizable. The abuse and violence followed a pattern called the cycle of abuse, described in chapter 1, "Were You in an Abusive Relationship?" In between episodes of abuse were periods of apparent harmony that made it easier to discount the abuse.

There were probably many factors that kept the relationship going and kept your love alive. There were all his promises. "I promise this will never happen again." You believed him the first time. And the second. As the abuse continued, he became increasingly remorseful, his promises more insistent. You continued to believe him; you wanted to believe him. After all, you loved him.

Then there were all the apologies. He seemed truly sorry. You forgave him. Now, however, when you think back, you realize the apologies were conditional. They blamed *you*! "I'm sorry, but if only you hadn't . . ." They always made his abuse somehow *your* fault. You may have begun to believe this, and you may even remember apologizing to *him*. You began to believe that if you were careful about what you said or did, you could prevent the abuse from happening again. As the abuse escalated over time, the blaming became more obvious. "I didn't mean to hurt you, but if you just weren't so [stupid, ugly, careless, dumb, etc.], this would never have happened." Time after time you were made to believe that every act of violence or abuse was your fault. Day after day you were made to feel that you were unworthy of him.

To convince you further that you were at fault, he probably told you that he never behaved this way with any previous partner (almost surely not true). You may have known someone he was with in the past who never said a word about abuse or violence. Therefore, you were inclined to believe that it must be something about you, and *he* is the one suffering from your failure to love him properly. *You* are the one who has to change somehow.

"If you really loved me . . ." Did you hear this a lot? Throughout your time together he used this and similar statements to let you know that if you only had the capacity to love him enough, the relationship would work. He explained that if he was abusive, it was because you didn't have the capacity to love him. You may have begun to believe this. But it wasn't *him* you were loving less, it was *you*.

All this sounds so horrible that you may have asked yourself, "Why didn't I leave sooner?" Well, as he was making you feel unworthy of him, he was also working to make you feel you were unworthy of everyone else too, that it would be impossible for you to find anyone else to love you. So, you stayed and tried to behave in ways that would please him and circumvent the abuse.

Perhaps you did try to discuss with others your growing doubts about this man and this relationship. You probably did not receive much support. Most abusers are very skilled at keeping that part of themselves hidden from the outside world. Others may have seen him as a charming, great guy and implied that you should try harder to make the relationship work. They were not willing to blame him, so again you thought it must be you who was "unlovable."

At those times he admitted to treating you poorly (if he ever made such an admission), he may have placed the blame on his past, on being abused as a child. He may even have asked you for help in recovering from his trauma. Again, he placed the responsibility on *you* to heal *him*. He may have blamed his abuse on other outside factors such as a bad day at work, finances, or someone else who made him angry. You may have felt sorry for him and believed that if you didn't try to help, you must not really love him. This became another justification for loving him. He needed you, and once you helped him heal, he would stop abusing you.

Another complicating factor is that certain cultural norms or religious teachings reinforce the notion that women should love their partner no matter what. In some cultures, it is the woman who is held responsible for the success or failure of a relationship. In others, abuse is seen not as unjust at all, but something a woman must endure. Your partner may even have used these beliefs against you, citing religious or other materials to justify his violent behavior (see chapter 1, "Were You in an Abusive Relationship?"). If you were raised with such beliefs, they will tend to interfere with recognizing that the abuse was wrong. They may have made it more difficult to stop loving him and may even have strengthened your need to continue loving him.

You spent a long time loving your abuser before you finally realized just how bad the situation was. Then you probably spent more time hoping and believing things would change. Next you believed it was all your fault. It's unrealistic to think that these feelings will disappear overnight. All the justifications, rationalizations, and excuses you used and believed for so long became part of your perception of yourself and him. It will take some more time now to readjust to your new life and new reality.

Every time you wonder how you could have loved such a person at all, much less still love him, stop to consider what it says about you as a loving person. If you didn't love him so much, this would not be so difficult. Despite what he told you, this shows how deeply you can care for another. It is time for you to become strong, to love yourself as much as you can love a partner. Now that you are free of the abuse, you can begin to re-create the love for yourself that he stole from you. This, in turn, will help you become a person who will be treated by your next partner with as much love and respect as you will offer him (see chapter 17, "Loving Again").

Why You Loved Him

You know that there were some positive things about your ex-partner that made you love him. If you are condemning yourself about your past and perhaps present feelings, it can be helpful to remember why you loved him.

When you are finished with this exercise, go back and review your answers in the chapter 1 self-exploration, Abusive Behaviors Inventory. Comparing these two lists should help remind you there were characteristics that made you love him and many that made it necessary for you to leave.

List the characteristics that originally attracted you to your ex-partner.

1. _____

2. _____

3. _____

4. _____

5. _____

6. _____

7. _____

8. _____

9. _____

10. _____

Now compare this list with your answers to the exercise at the end of chapter 1, Abusive Behaviors Inventory.

6
Losing Your Partner, Your Dream, Your Life

I knew I had done the right thing. Everyone kept telling me how it was such a good thing to leave him. If it was so good, why did it hurt so much?

ELLEN, AGE 29

We had plans. I had visions of a wonderful life together. I'm glad I'm out, but now I wonder if I'll ever have the life I imagined.

JAYNE, AGE 19

Myth: Losing an abusive partner isn't painful; it's a relief.

Myth: Dealing with the loss of an abusive relationship is much easier than losing a healthy relationship.

Whenever you end a relationship, you experience pain. Even if the breakup was your idea, it still hurts. After you got yourself out of the abusive relationship, you may have been surprised how sad you felt. Thinking of the relief you would feel to be out (and it *was* a relief) may have led you to believe it wouldn't be painful at all.

But it was. The pain may not have surfaced for days, weeks, months, or sometimes even years after the relationship ended.

If you are like most women who have left an abusive relationship, you may be feeling a sadness and loss just as acute as if a healthy relationship had ended. The loss of an intimate relationship, even a bad one, involves pain on a number of levels. It is not just the loss of a partner; it is much more.

You Lost a Lover and Companion

You didn't lose just a partner; you lost a lover and companion. If your sexual life with your partner was good, you probably miss the physical pleasure. Also, you may miss simply having a physically intimate relationship in your life: someone to hold you; to be physically near you; to kiss you hello or goodnight. You may miss holding someone's hand as you walk and sleeping next to someone at night.

You may also miss having someone to accompany you through all of the daily highs and lows. Not having someone to mull things over with at night or get a second opinion from may also leave a hole in your life.

You Lost Your Sexual "Innocence"

Sexual "innocence" does not refer to sexual inexperience or a naiveté about sex; it refers to feeling comfortable and trusting with a partner. If your relationship was sexually abusive, you experienced a different kind of sexual loss: the loss of feeling like a sexually healthy person. He took control over your body and took your sexuality away from you. No one has the right to take that from another person.

If you feel you are mourning the loss of your sexual innocence, that's a perfectly normal reaction. That your body is your own and *you* determine what and how and when you will have sex was taken away from you. He took away being able to trust potential partners. All of this he stole from you, and you have every right to mourn such a loss.

Your Lost Sexual Feeling

If your partner sexually assaulted you, he may have destroyed your ability to feel sexual in a positive, loving way. It may take a long time before you begin to experience the sexual side of yourself once again. Even when those feelings of sensuality and sexuality do return, you may experience great difficulty having sex with your next partner. Intimacy with someone new may trigger memories and sensations of the horrors or the abuse. This may cause you to avoid sexual situations completely until you are able to move past those memories. This is a normal reaction to your abuse history and a clear reason to feel a great sense of loss.

Although less common, an opposite reaction may occur in some survivors of sexual abuse. In rare cases, some women may become much more sexual with a greater number of partners than before the abuse as a way of trying to deal with the violence they experienced. Unfortunately, this also exposes them to further emotional or physical harm.

You Lost a Roommate

Along with losing a sexual partner, you may have lost someone with whom you could discuss daily events, thoughts, and issues in your life. For months or maybe years you may have had someone to talk to about personal problems, finances, the children, and daily activities. Now, you may miss having someone there to talk to when you get home.

If discussions of issues such as finances, attitudes, or other activities tended to create abusive episodes, you may be experiencing a very different sort of loss. If you were afraid to initiate discussions because of the potentially abusive results, you may still find yourself avoiding these discussions with people now. You may forgo talking to others, particularly a new partner, about anything that feels like an old "trigger."

If the abuse has caused you to feel anxious about being open and direct with others, this is another very real loss. Your ability to be assertive and speak your mind without fear of violence is a terrible sacrifice. It may feel as though a very important part of you was stolen.

You Lost a Confidant

When a relationship ends, you often lose someone who was, at least in some ways, a confidant. Regardless of the abuse, you may have talked with your ex-partner about things you didn't discuss with anyone else. You may have discussed daily, routine events or personal, intimate issues, but when the relationship ended, your confidant was gone.

Even though you know your decision to leave was the right one, you may experience profound loneliness. Losing a sexual partner, a confidant, someone you were planning your life with leaves a large hole in your life. Despite the abuse you endured, and your knowledge that you had to get out, you may still experience these feelings of loss. This sorrow does not mean that the relationship wasn't unhealthy; you know it was. Nor does it imply that you really wanted or needed to be in an abusive relationship; you know that's not true. It just means you feel the loss of some of the better elements of your relationship.

You Lost a Part of Yourself

Have you sensed that you are not the same person you were before the abuse? Survivors often talk about losing parts of their personalities. Friends and family may have mentioned how different you seem now. If you were outgoing, assertive, or carefree before the abuse, you may feel that you are now more withdrawn, passive, and rigid. Perhaps you detect other new undesirable characteristics such as excessive anger, pessimism, or a general distrust of others.

It's not difficult to understand how the trauma you experienced could be powerful enough to produce sweeping and fundamental changes in you. You have undoubtedly added these changes to the losses you are mourning. Chances are good, however, that the "real you" has not been permanently lost. Over time you will begin to see glimpses of those healthy, positive traits reappearing.

Eventually, you will probably be able to recapture the person you used to be, and maybe even improve upon her!

You Lost Your Valued Possessions

During your relationship your ex-partner may have damaged or destroyed some of your most treasured personal belongings. Often, an abuser will destroy, sell, or toss out specific possessions he knows you prize the most. You may have lost some irreplaceable items that had great sentimental value for you. This is one more weapon in his arsenal of control and manipulation. He may have smashed objects during his violent episodes, or you may have noticed items broken or missing when you returned home late or following an evening out with friends of whom he didn't approve. In addition, when you left your abuser, it's possible you had to abandon many valued personal effects.

If you and your partner shared expenses, such as mortgage payment or rent, utilities, food, or car payments, or if he brought in most or all of the family income, you lost a large part of your economic security as well. Often such a loss can make you feel insecure and unsafe.

It is natural to mourn these losses. Although your treasures can never be replaced, you now are able to protect the cherished belongings in your life. You can be confident that no one will be able to take them from you again.

You Lost Your Life's Dream

You also may be mourning the profound loss of a dream. When you began the relationship with this man, you may have felt that he was *the* one. You may have envisioned a life together forever. You may have planned to marry him, have children, and build a life with him. You may feel a sense of great loss for the dream you once thought you shared with him.

You may have lost many other dreams along the way. Your dreams of owning a home, living in a community as an intact, happy family, being in a longtime, secure relationship. You are mourning all these losses. Knowing it was good and right to leave should not in any way diminish allowing yourself to grieve. You know now that your dream could never have become reality, but the loss makes you sad nonetheless.

You Lost Your Dreams for Children

If you envisioned that your life with him included children, but this didn't happen, you may be wondering when, if ever, you will have your family. Your experience of abuse may have altered your thoughts about having kids in the future. Maybe you chose not to bring children into such an abusive atmosphere, but now you wonder if you will ever feel comfortable enough in a relationship to give birth in the future. This may be another source of grief for you.

If you had children with your ex-partner, you probably assumed at the time that you were in a stable relationship. You may have believed that relationship would provide a father for your children. This assumption was also shattered by his abuse.

Perhaps you had to leave your children behind to escape the violence. If this is so, then your grief and loss are magnified. But remember how important it was to get away. Witnessing the abuse over and over may have been more unhealthy for your children than being separated from you temporarily (see chapter 10, "What About the Children?"). If you had stayed, and your partner's violence escalated to murder, your children would have lost their mom forever. If you are not able to be in contact with your children now, you hope you will be able to see them soon (see chapter 12, "Practical Considerations").

You may also be mourning the loss of a healthy upbringing for your children. One of the most difficult legacies of an abusive relationship is the sense of loss you feel for your children. Along with this may be the guilt of exposing your children to your former partner for as long as you did. Again, you didn't see the abuse coming. You were doing what you needed to do to survive. It is easy in hindsight to see what you might have done differently. But if leaving sooner had risked your life or theirs, there is no question that you did what was best for them.

If your children witnessed the abuse you endured, you are now feeling the loss of their innocence too. If your former partner directly abused your children, you are grieving for that as well. No matter what the particulars were, if you believe that your children sacrificed parts of their childhood because of this abusive relationship, it makes perfect sense that you would mourn their losses.

You Lost Part of Your Family

When you left the abusive relationship there were probably others whom you lost in addition to a partner. You may have developed close ties to some of his family members, but now have no connection whatsoever. There probably were friends of his you thought were yours too. But they either knew nothing about the abuse or refused to believe you about it. They remained loyal to him but deserted you when the relationship ended. And if you needed to hide from your former partner, you may have lost everyone.

How did your family and friends react when your relationship ended? If they were not understanding and supportive, you may have lost them too. Perhaps they failed to support you because they refused to believe the abuse was occurring or because they felt that it was your duty to stay with your partner. Their reactions and attitudes to your ordeal may eliminate any possibility of your feeling close to them now. They may have thought they were being supportive, but their actions and words were not helpful. So you may have chosen to separate yourself from them (see chapter 11, "The Reactions of Others"). Even if the distancing was your decision, your sense of loss is not diminished.

You Lost Your Job

If you had to move away to escape your abuser, you probably had to leave your job. You may even have sacrificed your career. You worked hard to get where you were, to establish a good reputation at work, perhaps to advance up the ranks. After leaving your position, it may have been difficult for you to reestablish yourself in the work world. Being forced to start all over again professionally can create profound feelings of loss.

The Pain of Loss

After considering all the possible reasons *why* you may be grieving, it is important to examine what this grieving feels like. Elizabeth Kübler-Ross, the famous researcher on loss, grief, and death, discussed in her book *On Death and Dying*[1] the stages experienced by someone who is dying or has lost a loved one. These stages can easily be adapted to the loss you experienced when your relationship ended.

Kübler-Ross's stages of grieving do not always follow a predictable pattern. This is particularly true if you are grieving the loss of an abusive relationship. Your loss is very complicated and may alter not only the pattern of the stages but the length and intensity of each stage.

The first stage discussed by Kübler-Ross is shock or *denial*. Even though you may have been planning the demise of your relationship for a long time, it may seem unreal when it finally happens. It may take a while before you can wake up in the morning with the clear realization that you are out. You may find you maintain patterns of behavior as if you are still in the relationship. Eventually, however, this denial will disappear.

Another stage of loss you probably experienced was *anger*. It is much safer to allow yourself to feel your anger when you are free of the danger of the relationship. If you had allowed yourself to feel this anger while you were with him, it might have created an even worse situation for you. Submitting to your partner's demands would have become unbearable if your anger surfaced. And not submitting might have made him far more dangerous.

Now that you are out, you can allow yourself to feel the anger. But instead of feeling anger about a single, recent episode of violence, you may now feel all your anger rise up at once (see

[1] Kubler-Ross, E. (1969). *On death and dying*. New York: Simon and Schuster.

chapter 7, "When Feelings Overwhelm You"). Some of this anger may be directed at yourself. You may blame yourself for allowing such a relationship to happen to you, for not getting out sooner, for not standing up for yourself. These are perfectly normal feelings, but try to keep in mind that you did the best you could to survive.

Depression is another stage in the grieving process. Sadness, tearfulness, disrupted sleep patterns, and poor concentration are signs of the depression that often appear after an abusive relationship. These symptoms may progress into a deeper, more profound depression. Again, this is a normal reaction to the abuse and there are ways of treating your depression (see chapter 13, "Beginning to Heal").

Finally, gradually, over many months and perhaps years, you may come to the stage of grieving called *acceptance*. This doesn't simply mean accepting that the relationship is over. It means you no longer are reacting to the abuse as if it were still part of your daily life. It means being able to work through the pain this relationship left you with and moving on. Even if this seems impossible to you right now, it will happen. It won't happen easily or quickly, but sometime in the future the abuse will no longer be such a painful part of your everyday life.

Coping with the Losses

Overcoming loss is a slow process. One of the worst things you can do is to hurry it. There may be many others who will expect you to "cheer up and be happy" and get on with life. They will say things like, "You should be feeling great; you're out!" But they are only seeing that you got out of a bad relationship. They are not in a position to see all the related losses that you are suffering.

Only you know the healing you have to do and how long it will take. If you are worrying that the grieving process is going on too long, think about how long you loved and believed in your partner. If you loved him for years, then believing the pain should be over in a few weeks or a month is unrealistic. If you rush your healing, you might end up merely burying the pain only to find it resurfacing in the future.

You need to allow yourself to feel bad. If you have one of those days when you are tearful all day, that's OK. Crying is not a sign of weakness, nor is it silly. It means that you are allowing yourself to feel. Until you allow yourself to experience the emotions of that loss, you can't begin the healing process.

Find someone whom you can talk to about how you are feeling. Make sure it is someone who is going to listen without judging you, someone who can understand that no matter how abusive the relationship was, there are still many losses you must mourn. He or she must be willing to stick with you through your grieving and not try to hurry you.

Often in abusive relationships, there are many things left unsaid. You probably weren't able to tell your ex-partner everything you would like to tell him. You may have stayed silent because of the potential for further abuse or because your feelings fell on deaf ears. It's important to be able to vent your feelings even if you can't tell him directly (see the exercise at the end of this chapter).

Reading books and articles about loss can help. This is another means of sharing your feelings with others. Reading about others who have gone through what you are experiencing can make you feel less alone with your pain. (see "Resources," at the end of this book).

Meeting with a counselor or therapist who understands how painful and difficult this is for you can help, too. A counselor can help you allow yourself to grieve without judgment or self-recrimination. Venting to someone else about your pain can, all by itself, help to heal (see chapter 13, "Beginning to Heal").

Expressing Your feelings

You probably have not been able to tell your abuser how you feel about what he did to you. Releasing some of your feelings toward him can be a very therapeutic experience. Set aside at least an hour for this exercise (or more if you think you need it). In the space below (and on as many more sheets of paper as you need) write a letter to your abuser. You will *not* send this letter to your abuser, so feel free to write everything you have ever wanted to say to him. Take your time. There is no right or wrong way to do it. The outline below offers some suggestions for thoughts you might want to include in your letter. Feel free to use it as a guideline or write the letter in your own words if that feels more comfortable.

Dear_____,

1. Purpose of writing.

2. How he made you feel.

3. What losses you have felt due to his abuse.

4. Other feelings, such as shock, anger, and depression. Explain what they are like and how he caused them.

5. Any other feelings about him and the abuse.

When you are done with your letter, set it aside. Put it in a place where you won't see it on a daily basis. While the letter is away, notice any new thoughts that come to mind about what you wish you could have said to him. When these thoughts occur, get the letter out and edit it. Keep adding to your letter until you find that at least 1 week has gone by without any new additions.

The next step is to decide what to do with your letter. If you find that you are not ready to part with it, that's OK. Put it away until you decide it is time to get it out of your life.

When you do decide it's time, make a ritual out of the destroying of the letter. Think about what would feel right to you: ripping it up into a million little pieces, burying it, burning it, or some combination of these. Decide if you want to do this alone or accompanied by a trusted friend. Do not be surprised by your reactions when you destroy the letter: Relief, anger, satisfaction, or sadness are all possible and normal.

If you find that this exercise is helpful, but more thoughts and feelings emerge over time, repeat the process. As always, there is no right or wrong way to do this, but you should find this exercise very therapeutic.

7

When Feelings Overwhelm You

I feel so bad all the time. It can't be normal to be so upset after getting out.

ALLISON, AGE 17

Everyone keeps telling me I did nothing wrong. I guess I know that's true. It still feels as though it was my fault somehow. It feels as if I hurt myself and hurt everyone else around me.

MANDY, AGE 28

Myth: The emotional turmoil you experience in the aftermath of an abusive relationship is brief and usually fairly mild.

Myth: All survivors experience very similar emotions after leaving an abusive relationship.

*I*t's easy to imagine that emotions such as fear, anxiety, anger, and depression arising from an abusive relationship would quickly subside when you are finally away from your abuser. Yet nothing could be further from the truth. Many, if not all, of those debili-

tating feelings can linger for months or even years, and new undesirable emotions may appear in the aftermath of the abuse.

Healing requires you to understand that these ongoing feelings
are normal and will diminish over time, either through your own
efforts or, in some cases, with outside help such as counseling.
While every abused woman's emotional struggles will be different,
let's look at the most common and, often, most difficult ones.

Fear

Removing yourself from your abuser does not mean that your fear
is gone. Many women who have escaped violent partners know the
danger that follows them beyond the relationship. You are the best
judge of how safe you are. Be sure to read chapter 2, "Are You Out
of Danger Now?", and take whatever steps are necessary to
increase your safety.

Many people don't understand why you are still afraid *after* the
relationship. You know all too well that your partner may not stop
the abuse and violence just because you left. In fact, it may escalate.
You know he was not always rational. Even if it means risking
arrest and jail by violating a restraining order, he may still try to
hurt you. So it is *perfectly normal* for you to continue to be afraid.

Your abuser may not have overtly threatened or attempted to
kill you, but, nevertheless, you may have been in fear for your life.
When a partner acts irrationally and impulsively, it becomes
impossible to predict what he may do next. If the abuse in your
relationship slowly intensified over time, you logically assumed it
would continue to increase. Remember, he did so many unbeliev-
able things to you. How could you *not* live in fear of all the other
unimaginable acts of which he was capable?

What if you know, intellectually, there is no reason for you to
be fearful now, and yet you are? Perhaps you have moved and your
abuser has no way of finding you. Maybe he's in jail or deceased.
You *know*, at least for now, that you are not in any real danger.
However, many reasons exist for your fear.

Chances are you lived with fear in your relationship for a long time. The fear you experienced may not have been based solely on the threat of being killed. It may have been the fear of physical, verbal, or emotional assault. Fear may have become a "normal" part of your very "not normal" daily life.

Now that you are out of that abusive situation, do you continue to experience fear when an event occurs that used to "set him off"? Many common, daily occurrences probably activated his terrible, violent cycle. Now that you are out, these daily events don't lead to abuse, but your mind and body have been conditioned to associate them with the violence. So when one of these triggers occurs, your automatic emotional and physical response is fear. Keep in mind: It took time for this fear to be conditioned in you and it may take almost as long for you to "unlearn" these associations. Just as you learned these defense mechanisms gradually, you will unlearn them gradually.

Guilt

You know the abuse wasn't your fault. You know you did everything you could to prevent and, finally, to end the abuse. You know you did what was necessary to survive that relationship. You didn't do anything wrong! *So why do you still feel guilty?*

Guilt is one of those very sneaky emotions. Intellectually, you know you have no reason to feel guilty and yet, there it is. You can tell yourself the guilt will do you no good, but it persists. Experiencing guilt after leaving an abusive relationship can be one of the most confusing emotions.

So, again, why do you feel guilty? The best way to understand this is to determine the source of your original guilt. Usually, the "bait" for your guilt was set before the relationship even began.

Do you remember your former partner using subtle forms of guilt to get you into the relationship at the very beginning? Maybe he complained that you were unfair to refuse to go out with him. Perhaps he told you how terribly his feelings would be hurt if you refused him. Can you remember how he found a way to make you feel you were doing something *wrong* if you didn't begin a relationship with him?

Once he got you into the relationship, his use of guilt increased. If you didn't want to do what he wanted, when he wanted to do it, he made you feel you had done something *wrong*. Anytime you had an opinion that differed from his, he found a way to leave you feeling your opinion was *wrong* and you were *wrong* to have disagreed with him. He may have reinforced this guilt by telling you how much he loved you and only wanted what was best for you. If you resisted or disagreed with him, he claimed you were hurting him deeply and you just didn't understand the true depths of his love.

Guilt was a very powerful tool for seizing control over you. He won a major battle when he established a pattern of making you feel at fault whenever you disagreed or opposed him in any way. Think back on the relationship. Do you remember feeling at fault and guilty whenever problems arose in the relationship? Do you remember feeling guilty even when you knew it was in no way your fault? These feelings become ingrained and do not simply evaporate when you are free of the relationship.

Your abuser may have blamed you for situations that were obviously no one's fault. This may have happened when circumstances were beyond anyone's control: The car broke down, the toilet backed up, the kids got sick. Although you were in no way responsible for these occurrences, you still got blamed. Not only was the problem blamed on you, the abuse that often followed was blamed on you as well.

He may have blamed you for things that did not even exist. A common example of this is the extreme jealousy abusers often exhibit. If your partner was excessively jealous, he may have blamed and abused you for nonexistent flirting with another man. Again, you were made to feel guilty when you had done nothing wrong.

Finally, guilt was heaped on you for the fact that the abuse continued. How often after an abusive episode did you hear, "I'm sorry, but if only you hadn't . . ." This was the ultimate guilt tactic. *He made you responsible for your own abuse.* Therefore, you felt it was your fault.

When guilt is so deeply instilled in you, whether it stems solely from this abusive relationship or grows out of other experiences in your past as well, it is difficult to let it go. It takes time to get past the guilt, no matter how vicious and traumatic the abuse you endured. Now that you are out, you may find it easy to take on new guilt. You may find yourself thinking, "If only I hadn't . . ." Hindsight can be painful, especially when it involves berating yourself for actions you couldn't control. The more you heal from the abuse, the easier it will be to release yourself from your guilt. Some of the techniques discussed in chapter 9, "Managing Your Stress," such as "thought stopping," may help you to move beyond guilt-related feelings.

Unreleased Anger

What about the anger? Is your anger still buried although it's been weeks, months, or years since your abusive relationship? Perhaps others have asked you why you don't appear angry with your abuser. People may even have been encouraging you to "let your anger out!" It makes perfect sense to be angry, enraged even, after what he did, but you just don't feel it. The truth may be that you just don't feel it *yet*. Your outward acceptance of what he did to you may end one of these days and you may find yourself exploding with rage.

You concealed your anger for so long, it may take years before you are ready to express it. You may be afraid of releasing your anger, of losing control. Hiding your anger was a defense mechanism that served you well with your abuser. It was one of many strategies you used to survive in that relationship. After a while it became routine. You may have learned this "trick" so well, unlearning it is difficult.

What do you think will happen if you release all your anger? You may fear the anger will be uncontrollable if you allow it to escape. Or you may worry you will never be able to move past it. Once you begin to express the anger, it may feel somewhat overpowering for a while, but you will move beyond it. Your anger will not destroy you (see the following section, Anger Released). If you are truly afraid to release your anger, you may need a counselor's help to feel safe enough to express your most powerful emotions.

Perhaps you are afraid that if you release your anger, you will direct it at people who don't deserve it. However, those who know you and are aware of your past know that anger is a normal reaction to the abuse. If you were to express your anger and some of it was misdirected toward them, they would probably understand, support you, and possibly feel relieved that your anger was finally emerging. If you find that some misplaced anger upsets a friend or family member, talk to them afterward about what happened. Apologize and explain that you are still working through some of your emotions from the abuse. Being open and honest with them should help to smooth out any hurt feelings.

Good friends will not blame you, abandon you, or judge you for doing something you need to do: vent your anger. If your anger surfaces often or becomes too intense for your friendships and other relationships to bear, then it may be time to think about getting outside help. Chapter 13 can assist you in finding such outside supports.

Anger Released

On the other hand, once you were out and safe, all of that stored-up anger may have exploded all at once. For many people, once that stockpile of stored anger begins to erupt, capping it is difficult or impossible. Anger may have controlled your life for a while and you found it difficult to feel anything except angry.

Anger directed at your abuser is, of course, one of the most normal reactions a person can have. But as with any emotion, anger can sometimes rise to extreme levels. You may have been so angry with him you wanted to hurt him back just as he hurt you. Perhaps you have elaborate fantasies about strategies for exacting vengeance on him emotionally and physically.

Thoughts of hurting or even killing your abuser are not wrong or dangerous in themselves. Most survivors have such thoughts at one time or another. But if you suspect you may act on your fantasies in ways that will end up hurting *you* (criminal acts, behaviors that could jeopardize child custody, risking direct retaliation from him, etc.), safer and more effective ways exist to release your anger (see chapter 13, "Beginning to Heal").

Depression

Since you left your abuser, have you felt very down, sad, and fatigued for no obvious reason? Have your eating and sleeping patterns changed significantly? Do you feel your situation is hopeless? Have you lost interest in your favorite activities? These are common signs and symptoms of depression.

Depression is perhaps the most common emotional experience for women in the aftermath of an abusive relationship. Once you are out, you can contemplate the relationship in ways that weren't possible when you were in it. Although in the long run you may find such reflection to be very desirable and helpful in your healing process, it can also create a great sense of sadness and loss.

As mentioned in chapter 6, "Losing Your Partner, Your Dream, Your Life," you suffered many losses because of the abuse. These losses create great sadness and often serious depression similar to the experience of loss when a loved one dies. It is difficult to imagine how anyone could experience what you did and not feel profound sadness and sorrow. Grief and depression over your losses are perfectly normal. But severe depression can be terribly debilitating and can create barriers to your healing process. So it's important for you to be aware of depression's signs and symptoms.

Some signs that are relatively easy to spot involve major changes in your daily habits. If your eating pattern has changed and you find yourself seriously overeating or undereating, this could be a symptom of depression. The same is true for your sleeping habits. Depression is frequently characterized by insomnia, difficulty going to sleep, frequent awakenings during the night, waking in the early morning and being unable to go back to sleep, or a combination of these symptoms. On the other hand, you may find that you are sleeping considerably more than usual. And though your amount of sleep is far greater than before, you find you are always exhausted. Sleep may have become a welcome escape from the echoes of the abuse, but it's also a frequent sign of depression.

Other common indicators of depression are feelings of hopelessness, overwhelming sadness, a belief that your life will never improve, thoughts that you really don't deserve better, and, most disturbing, thoughts of hurting or killing yourself.

It's important to look at your history of depression. If you exhibited a pattern of depression before the abusive relationship, be sure to consider that now. It's possible your depression may go deeper than your current healing process. Preexisting depression, especially if it has been characteristic of your life in the past, might be something you need to discuss with your doctor or a therapist to determine appropriate treatment.

Everyone becomes depressed at times. If you are a survivor of an abusive relationship, you have every reason to feel depressed. Denying or suppressing your depression is unhealthy. However, if you are concerned about your depression and it seems to have lasted too long or is particularly severe, you may want to do some self-evaluation to get an idea of just how serious it is.

One way is to give some thought to how long you have felt depressed. The length of time depression should last following an abusive relationship varies a great deal. You cannot expect, and others should not expect, that your depression *should* last a matter of weeks or months. You went through a great deal of trauma, and as we have said often, healing is not immediate.

Although it is difficult to say exactly how long is too long for depression to last, you can examine the course of your depression for clues to how you are doing. Do you feel worse than you did a month or two ago? Is the depression beginning to interfere with your relationships with others, your job, or other parts of your daily life? Are you increasingly unable to accomplish everyday tasks? Overall, do you feel that your mood is not improving? Improvement does not imply that your depression is gone. It means you can identify minutes, hours, or perhaps a day when you feel less depressed than last week or last month. If you feel you are becoming less depressed, that your depressive "episodes" are decreasing in frequency and duration, you are probably on the right track, but you still want to be attentive to your moods.

The most important time to be concerned about depression is when it is accompanied by thoughts of killing yourself. The fear, anger, and depression that surface in the aftermath of the abuse can make you feel so terrible you just don't want to face them. Your abuser made you feel so bad for so long, the pain may just feel too great. This is especially true if you believed your life would be instantly transformed when you left him. Now, the reality of this difficult time transition and the amount of work still to do may feel overwhelmingly oppressive and hopeless. Those feelings can turn a depressed person into a suicidal one.

If you are having thoughts of suicide, *get help*. As difficult as it may be to believe now, things *will* get better. It takes time for your emotions to surface and run their course. You've accomplished a great deal; giving up now is shortchanging yourself. You deserve to live a happy, abuse-free life. It *can* happen. Again, it will just take time (see chapter 13, "Beginning to Heal"). Consider finding someone supportive to help you through this difficult process. Talking with a therapist should not be embarrassing. Again, your feelings are justified. Allowing someone to help you shows great inner strength and courage. Friends and family members can probably listen and offer support, but they are not trained to help you through your depression. Calling on professionals for this is the greatest stride you can take toward healing.

Anger Turned Inward: Self-Injurious Behavior

Following an abusive relationship, some women find that they have an overpowering urge to hurt themselves. This feeling can be one of the most difficult to admit to anyone. If you have felt this way and have shared these feelings with others, their responses may not have been as supportive or helpful as you had hoped.

They were probably shocked. They may have expressed their feeling that having endured enough pain and violence in your relationship, you must be crazy to want to hurt yourself more.

You are *not* crazy. Victims of abuse may physically hurt themselves for a number of psychological reasons. Many survivors say they experience a period of emotional numbness. It is frightening to feel nothing at all and even more scary to think you may never feel anything ever again. Numbness is an effective defense mechanism that helps to keep emotions from overwhelming you. Hurting yourself (cutting, scratching, burning, etc.) may be a way of testing your senses and reassuring yourself you can indeed "feel" something. Feelings will come back to you in time. The numbness will eventually subside. You may not be ready to experience the full force of your emotions yet.

Another reason for self-harm is an attempt to regain some control over your body and life. For so long, your abuser exerted control over your body. His strategies for this may have included objectifying you, degrading your appearance, sexual assault, or rape. He also controlled other aspects of your life: where you went, who you saw, what you did. Self-injurious behaviors may be your way of reclaiming the personal control you lost.

Some survivors of violent relationships develop a learned association between anxiety and pain. In your relationship, tension and anxiety usually preceded the violent episodes. Now that you are out, you may still have a strong mental connection between anxiety and pain. In your relationship, waiting for the violence to happen was, at times, unbearable. There still may be the desire to get the anxiety or fear over and done with.

Your abuser went to great lengths to convince you of what a bad person you are. It may take you some time to let go of your negative self-concepts stemming from his actions. Injuring yourself may serve, in your mind, to prove how bad you are.

Whatever the reasons for hurting yourself, you may feel embarrassed or ashamed to admit it to anyone. If you wish to deal with these feelings and behaviors, you may need to work with a counselor who is specifically trained in working with self-injurious behaviors. This counselor will not judge you or think you are crazy. He or she will work with you to recognize the origins of the behavior and help you deal with it.

Post Traumatic Stress Disorder

If you lived through a particularly abusive relationship, you may suffer from what is called *post traumatic stress disorder* (PTSD). This disorder may be familiar to you in the context of veterans of wars. You may have heard about veterans who continue to experience reactions to the violence and horror they experienced in battle, long after the war ended.

Psychologists have found that veterans of wars are not the only group vulnerable to PTSD. It appears that anyone who lives through extreme violence of various kinds may suffer from PTSD. Does it seem to you that you lived through your own personal war? Was there a reason to be afraid a great deal of the time? Was life continually unpredictable with negative consequences no matter what you did? Did you experience abuse and violence that no person should ever have to endure?

One common symptom of PTSD is reacting more fearfully than others to startling events. When something alarming suddenly occurs, PTSD sufferers experience extreme responses such as heart palpitations, rapid breathing, and profuse sweating. Another characteristic of PTSD is the ominous feeling that something terrible is about to happen, although no real danger threat exists. Finally, if you are suffering from PTSD, you may find thoughts and images of the abuse suddenly jumping into your head for no reason. These images seem real, almost as if you are reliving them.

If you are suffering from post traumatic stress disorder, this doesn't mean that you are crazy or weak. It means you are having a normal reaction to a very abnormal ordeal in your life. Unfortunately, when you stop to think about it, many parallels exist between war and domestic violence. As with other emotions discussed in this chapter, PTSD symptoms will take time to subside. If you find that these symptoms are seriously interfering with your daily life, you may need to work with a counselor to overcome them. See chapter 8, "Signs of Healing," for further discussion of PTSD.

Other Intense Emotions

The specific feelings addressed in this chapter are shared by many women who have endured and survived an abusive or violent relationship. It is by no means an exhaustive list of the emotions that may be causing difficulty for you now. These powerful emotions are normal, predictable reactions to a terribly powerful episode in your life. Becoming aware of your emotions, giving yourself time to feel them, and finding the help you may need to deal with them will allow you to move beyond your troubling emotions to the healing and comforting feelings you deserve.

Assessing Your Feelings: Week One

Sometimes it is difficult to assess the seriousness of your emotional difficulties. It's also difficult to be objective about the extent to which your feelings are interfering with your life. If you push your feelings aside or try to minimize them, you risk becoming stuck in them. This is a weeklong self-exploration exercise. It takes some time and effort, so plan carefully and follow through with it. You will find it very helpful. If you find working on this exercise feels uncomfortable and anxiety-producing, you may need either to wait until you feel ready or to enlist the help of a counselor to support you while you explore your feelings.

In part I of the following chart, check off all the feelings that you are experiencing. In part II, document how often you are aware of the feelings during 1 week. In part III, use the scale to determine how disturbing and disruptive the feelings are at different times during the day. During this time, also work on the last section of the chart. In part IV, record each time your feelings of fear, anger, guilt, or depression interfered with your life. This exercise is designed to be repeated after 1 month so you can be aware of your progress.

Do not judge your feelings. No "right or wrong" feelings exist. This chart is simply a way for you to examine your feelings more closely.

Part I

Check the feelings you are experiencing now. Check all that apply to you.

____ Fear of continued violence by ex-partner
____ Fear of violence by another person
____ Other fear _____
____ Anger toward former partner
____ Anger toward yourself
____ Anger over circumstances that contributed to the abuse
____ Anger toward others who did not help
____ Anger toward others not related to the abuse

___ Anger over current problems not associated with the abuse
___ Other anger _____
___ Guilt over having begun the relationship
___ Guilt over having stayed in the relationship for as long as you did
___ Guilt over being unable to stop your partner's abuse
___ Other guilt _____
___ Feelings of sadness
___ Feelings of hopelessness
___ Change in eating patterns
___ Change in sleeping patterns
___ Thoughts of killing yourself
___ Other related feelings of depression
___ Thoughts of, or actual, cutting or other self-injury
___ Extreme reaction to sudden sounds or events
___ Thoughts of the abuse that suddenly jump into your mind
___ Inability to think about the abuse
___ Other _____
___ Other _____

♦ *Total number of items checked* _____

Part II

For 1 week, note approximately how many times each of the feelings occurs.

Feeling	Days experienced feeling (check all that apply)						
	MON	TUES	WED	THURS	FRI	SAT	SUN
Fear of continued violence by ex-partner	—	—	—	—	—	—	—
Fear of violence by another person	—	—	—	—	—	—	—
Other fear _____	—	—	—	—	—	—	—
Anger toward former partner	—	—	—	—	—	—	—
Anger toward yourself	—	—	—	—	—	—	—
Anger over circumstances that contributed to the abuse	—	—	—	—	—	—	—

	MON	TUES	WED	THURS	FRI	SAT	SUN
Anger toward others who did not help	__	__	__	__	__	__	__
Anger toward others not related to the abuse	__	__	__	__	__	__	__
Anger over current problems not associated with the abuse	__	__	__	__	__	__	__
Other anger _____	__	__	__	__	__	__	__
Guilt over having begun the relationship	__	__	__	__	__	__	__
Guilt over having stayed in the relationship for as long as you did	__	__	__	__	__	__	__
Guilt over being unable to stop your partner's abuse	__	__	__	__	__	__	__
Other guilt_____	__	__	__	__	__	__	__
Feelings of sadness	__	__	__	__	__	__	__
Feelings of hopelessness	__	__	__	__	__	__	__
Change in eating patterns	__	__	__	__	__	__	__
Change in sleeping patterns	__	__	__	__	__	__	__
Thoughts of killing yourself	__	__	__	__	__	__	__
Other related feelings of depression	__	__	__	__	__	__	__
Thoughts of, or actual, cutting or other self-injury	__	__	__	__	__	__	__
Extreme reaction to sudden sounds or events	__	__	__	__	__	__	__
Thoughts of the abuse that suddenly jump into your mind	__	__	__	__	__	__	__
Inability to think about the abuse	__	__	__	__	__	__	__

♦ *Number of feelings experienced every day of the week*
_____

♦ *Number of feelings experienced on 4 to 6 days during the week*
_____

♦ *Number of feelings experienced on only 1 to 3 days during the week*
_____

Part III

For each day, rate the severity of your feelings on a scale from 0 to 10, where 0 means the feeling did not occur at all that day and 10 means that the feeling was the most powerful and consuming you can imagine.

Feeling	Severity rating (0–10)						
	MON	TUES	WED	THURS	FRI	SAT	SUN
Fear of continued violence by ex-partner	__	__	__	__	__	__	__
Fear of violence by another person	__	__	__	__	__	__	__
Other fear _____	__	__	__	__	__	__	__
Anger toward former partner	__	__	__	__	__	__	__
Anger toward yourself	__	__	__	__	__	__	__
Anger over circumstances that contributed to the abuse	__	__	__	__	__	__	__
Anger toward others who did not help	__	__	__	__	__	__	__
Anger toward others not related to the abuse	__	__	__	__	__	__	__
Anger over current problems not associated with the abuse	__	__	__	__	__	__	__
Other anger _____	__	__	__	__	__	__	__
Guilt over having begun the relationship	__	__	__	__	__	__	__
Guilt over having stayed in the relationship for as long as you did	__	__	__	__	__	__	__
Guilt over being unable to stop your partner's abuse	__	__	__	__	__	__	__
Other guilt_____	__	__	__	__	__	__	__
Feelings of sadness	__	__	__	__	__	__	__
Feelings of hopelessness	__	__	__	__	__	__	__
Change in eating patterns	__	__	__	__	__	__	__
Change in sleeping patterns	__	__	__	__	__	__	__

	MON	TUES	WED	THURS	FRI	SAT	
Thoughts of killing yourself	—	—	—	—	—	—	—
Other related feelings of depression	—	—	—	—	—	—	—
Thoughts of, or actual, cutting or other self-injury	—	—	—	—	—	—	—
Extreme reaction to sudden sounds or events	—	—	—	—	—	—	—
Thoughts of the abuse that suddenly jump into your mind	—	—	—	—	—	—	—
Inability to think about the abuse	—	—	—	—	—	—	—

♦ *Number of feelings rated over 8* _____
♦ *Number of feelings rated from 5 to 7* _____
♦ *Number of feelings rated from 2 to 4* _____
♦ *Number of feelings rated less than 2* _____

Part IV

For each day, write down the feelings you experienced and how each affected your other emotions, attitudes, behaviors, and interactions with others.

Monday   Feeling _____ Effect _____

Feeling _____ Effect _____

Feeling _____ Effect _____

Tuesday   Feeling _____ Effect _____

Feeling _____ Effect _____

Feeling _____ Effect _____

Wednesday Feeling _____ Effect _____

Feeling _____ Effect _____

Feeling _____ Effect _____

Thursday	Feeling _____	Effect _____
	Feeling _____	Effect _____
	Feeling _____	Effect _____
Friday	Feeling _____	Effect _____
	Feeling _____	Effect _____
	Feeling _____	Effect _____
Saturday	Feeling _____	Effect _____
	Feeling _____	Effect _____
	Feeling _____	Effect _____
Sunday	Feeling _____	Effect _____
	Feeling _____	Effect _____
	Feeling _____	Effect _____

You will notice that this entire exercise is printed again on the following pages. You can increase the value of this self-assessment by repeating it after a month has passed since the first time you completed it. This will allow you to see changes and progress for better or for worse. If you find over the course of a month these feelings are having less power over you, that's great! You are healing. If you see little change or if they have gained more power, it might help you to decide to seek some professional help to move past them.

Assessing Your Feelings: Week Two (1 month later)

It's a month or so later. Repeat this assessment and see your progress. We'll repeat the instructions.

In part I of the following chart, check off all the feelings that you are experiencing. In part II, document how often you are aware of the feelings during 1 week. In part III, use the scale to determine how disturbing and disruptive the feelings are at different times during the day. During this time, also work on the last section of the chart. In part IV, record each time your feelings of fear, anger, guilt, or depression interfered with your life.

Do not judge your feelings. No right or wrong feelings exist. This chart is simply a way for you to examine your feelings more closely.

Part I

Check the feelings you are experiencing now. Check all that apply to you.

____ Fear of continued violence by ex-partner
____ Fear of violence by another person
____ Other fear _____
____ Anger toward former partner
____ Anger toward yourself
____ Anger over circumstances that contributed to the abuse
____ Anger toward others who did not help
____ Anger toward others not related to the abuse
____ Anger over current problems not associated with the abuse
____ Other anger _____
____ Guilt over having begun the relationship
____ Guilt over having stayed in the relationship for as long as you did
____ Guilt over being unable to stop your partner's abuse
____ Other guilt _____
____ Feelings of sadness
____ Feelings of hopelessness

___ Change in eating patterns
___ Change in sleeping patterns
___ Thoughts of killing yourself
___ Other related feelings of depression
___ Thoughts of, or actual, cutting or other self-injury
___ Extreme reaction to sudden sounds or events
___ Thoughts of the abuse that suddenly jump into your mind
___ Inability to think about the abuse
___ Other _____
___ Other _____

- ♦ *Total number of items checked* _____
- ♦ *Total number of items checked in part I*
  (*week one*) _____
- ♦ *Total decreased by* _____
- ♦ *Total increased by* _____

Part II

For 1 week, note approximately how many times each of the feelings occurs.

Feeling	Days experienced feeling (check all that apply)						
	MON	TUES	WED	THURS	FRI	SAT	SUN
Fear of continued violence by ex-partner	__	__	__	__	__	__	__
Fear of violence by another person	__	__	__	__	__	__	__
Other fear _____	__	__	__	__	__	__	__
Anger toward former partner	__	__	__	__	__	__	__
Anger toward yourself	__	__	__	__	__	__	__
Anger over circumstances that contributed to the abuse	__	__	__	__	__	__	__
Anger toward others who did not help	__	__	__	__	__	__	__
Anger toward others not related to the abuse	__	__	__	__	__	__	__

	MON	TUES	WED	THURS	FRI	SAT	SUN
Anger over current problems not associated with the abuse	___	___	___	___	___	___	___
Other anger _____	___	___	___	___	___	___	___
Guilt over having begun the relationship	___	___	___	___	___	___	___
Guilt over having stayed in the relationship for as long as you did	___	___	___	___	___	___	___
Guilt over being unable to stop your partner's abuse	___	___	___	___	___	___	___
Other guilt_____	___	___	___	___	___	___	___
Feelings of sadness	___	___	___	___	___	___	___
Feelings of hopelessness	___	___	___	___	___	___	___
Change in eating patterns	___	___	___	___	___	___	___
Change in sleeping patterns	___	___	___	___	___	___	___
Thoughts of killing yourself	___	___	___	___	___	___	___
Other related feelings of depression	___	___	___	___	___	___	___
Thoughts of, or actual, cutting or other self-injury	___	___	___	___	___	___	___
Extreme reaction to sudden sounds or events	___	___	___	___	___	___	___
Thoughts of the abuse that suddenly jump into your mind	___	___	___	___	___	___	___
Inability to think about the abuse	___	___	___	___	___	___	___

♦ *Number of feelings experienced every day of the week*

_____

♦ *Number of feelings experienced on 4 to 6 days during the week* _____

♦ *Number of feelings experienced on only 1 to 3 days during the week* _____

From part II (week one):

- *Number of feelings experienced all 7 days* _____
- *Number of feelings experienced 4–6 days* _____
- *Number of feelings experienced 1–3 days* _____

Change from week one:

- *Decrease in number of feelings experienced all 7 days*

  _____

- *Increase in number of feelings experienced all 7 days*

  _____

- *Decrease in number of feelings experienced 4–6 days*

  _____

- *Increase in number of feelings experienced 4–6 days*

  _____

- *Decrease in number of feelings experienced 1–3 days*

  _____

- *Increase in number of feelings experienced 1–3 days*

  _____

Part III

For each day, rate the severity of your feelings on a scale from 0 to 10, where 0 means the feeling did not occur at all that day and 10 means that the feeling was the most powerful and consuming you can imagine.

Feeling	Severity rating (0–10)						
	MON	TUES	WED	THURS	FRI	SAT	SUN
Fear of continued violence by ex-partner	—	—	—	—	—	—	—
Fear of violence by another person	—	—	—	—	—	—	—
Other fear _____	—	—	—	—	—	—	—
Anger toward former partner	—	—	—	—	—	—	—
Anger toward yourself	—	—	—	—	—	—	—

	MON	TUES	WED	THURS	FRI	SAT	SUN
Anger over circumstances that contributed to the abuse	___	___	___	___	___	___	___
Anger toward others who did not help	___	___	___	___	___	___	___
Anger toward others not related to the abuse	___	___	___	___	___	___	___
Anger over current problems not associated with the abuse	___	___	___	___	___	___	___
Other anger _____	___	___	___	___	___	___	___
Guilt over having begun the relationship	___	___	___	___	___	___	___
Guilt over having stayed in the relationship for as long as you did	___	___	___	___	___	___	___
Guilt over being unable to stop your partner's abuse	___	___	___	___	___	___	___
Other guilt_____	___	___	___	___	___	___	___
Feelings of sadness	___	___	___	___	___	___	___
Feelings of hopelessness	___	___	___	___	___	___	___
Change in eating patterns	___	___	___	___	___	___	___
Change in sleeping patterns	___	___	___	___	___	___	___
Thoughts of killing yourself	___	___	___	___	___	___	___
Other related feelings of depression	___	___	___	___	___	___	___
Thoughts of, or actual, cutting or other self-injury	___	___	___	___	___	___	___
Extreme reaction to sudden sounds or events	___	___	___	___	___	___	___
Thoughts of the abuse that suddenly jump into your mind	___	___	___	___	___	___	___
Inability to think about the abuse	___	___	___	___	___	___	___

- ♦ *Number of feelings rated 8–10* _____
- ♦ *Number of feelings rated 5–7* _____
- ♦ *Number of feelings rated 3–5* _____

From part III (week one):

- *Number of feelings rated 8–10* _____
- *Number of feelings rated 5–7* _____
- *Number of feelings rated 3–5* _____
- *Number of feelings rated 3–5* _____

- *Decrease in the number of feelings rated 8–10* _____
- *Increase in the number of feelings rated 8–10* _____
- *Decrease in the number of feelings rated 5–7* _____
- *Increase in the number of feelings rated 5–7* _____
- *Decrease in the number of feelings rated 3–5* _____
- *Increase in the number of feelings rated 3–5* _____

Part IV

For each day, write down the feelings you experienced and how each affected your other emotions, attitudes, behaviors, and interactions with others.

Monday   Feeling _____   Effect _____

             Feeling _____   Effect _____

             Feeling _____   Effect _____

Tuesday   Feeling _____   Effect _____

             Feeling _____   Effect _____

             Feeling _____   Effect _____

Wednesday Feeling _____   Effect _____

             Feeling _____   Effect _____

             Feeling _____   Effect _____

Thursday   Feeling _____   Effect _____

             Feeling _____   Effect _____

             Feeling _____   Effect _____

Friday	Feeling _____	Effect _____
	Feeling _____	Effect _____
	Feeling _____	Effect _____
Saturday	Feeling _____	Effect _____
	Feeling _____	Effect _____
	Feeling _____	Effect _____
Sunday	Feeling _____	Effect _____
	Feeling _____	Effect _____
	Feeling _____	Effect _____

So, how do your comparisons look? The hope is that you are seeing decreases, however slight, in number, frequency, severity, and effects of your destructive emotional responses. If you are, that means you're on the right track in your process of emotional healing. If they are staying about the same, but are not interfering too greatly with your daily life, maybe it will just take more time for you to move past them. If, however, you find that the number, frequency, or severity is increasing, you may want to consider some professional counseling to help you work through these emotions so you can get on with the healing process.

8

Signs of Unfinished Healing

It's been six months since I got out. My life has really improved since then. So, I don't understand why I still get so down on myself.

JACKIE, AGE 34

I left that horrible relationship almost ten years ago. I know I've had a hard time building new friendships and intimate relationships over the years, but I never thought it could be tied to something that happened so long ago.

CLAIRE, AGE 57

Myth: Once the abuse is in your past, you will spontaneously begin to feel good about yourself.

Myth: The end of an abusive relationship marks an automatic beginning of close and healthy relationships.

Myth: Your life and your attitudes will improve steadily and predictably in the aftermath of an abusive relationship.

*T*his chapter offers you an opportunity to assess just how much healing you need to do. It would be great if your self-esteem, emotional well-being, and relationships with others all bounced right back, but that usually doesn't happen. You will have good days and bad days, good weeks and bad weeks, good times and bad times. This doesn't mean that you are doing something wrong or you're a slow healer. It's normal. Every survivor heals at her own individual pace. No one heals overnight—no one.

Look at the Big Picture

First, make sure you have realistic expectations. There are no deadlines or schedules. You just need to know you are heading in the right direction *overall*. If you see you are doing better than you were a month or 2 ago, that's great. However, if your life is not improving or you perceive that you are feeling worse, that's a signal to think about evaluating your progress toward healing.

You probably believed once you freed yourself from that awful relationship, life would be much better. No more unpredictability. No more unwanted surprises. No more fear. Now you may be realizing that life is not as predictable as you had hoped. However, the uncertainty is coming from within you. Sometimes you are not sure how you will feel when you wake up in the morning, how you will make it through the day, how you will relate to others.

Many survivors expect a smooth, constant upward swing after an abusive relationship is over. They expect each day to be better than the one before. When this doesn't happen, they become discouraged, disheartened, and fearful about the future.

You probably notice some days are better than the day before. But there are also those days when you seem to be in a holding pattern: not worse, but not better. Then there are the days when you sink to new emotional lows. It's important for you to resist making these daily judgments about your life. It's much more helpful to look at your overall pattern of healing. Are you doing better than you were just after you left the relationship? If you can answer "yes" to that question, you are healing, and healing is what's important, not how fast it happens.

Emotional Signs: Self-Esteem

Think back to your life before the relationship. If you had other abusive relationships before the last one, try to think back to how you were before the first one. Try to remember how you felt about yourself. Did you believe that you deserved respect? Did you assume that you would find someone who would love you and treat you as well as you treated him? Did you think that you were intelligent, attractive, sensitive, and caring? Were you able to love someone else fully? Did you believe in your talents and skills? Did you see yourself as a worthy person?

How do you perceive yourself now? Do you still hold yourself in high esteem? Do you believe that you are capable of reaching your goals and enjoying a rewarding and fulfilling relationship?

If not, it's time to evaluate how the abusive relationship sabotaged your self-esteem. Everyone deserves a positive and healthy self-image. You should be able to believe in yourself completely and know that you deserve nothing but the best.

You can assess your self-esteem using various methods. One way is to look at your plans for the future. Where do you see yourself 5 years from now? Visualize what your life will be like: your work, your home, your family, and your friends. Take a minute and really try to imagine the details of your future life (refer back to the self-exploration exercise at the end of the introduction).

How did your future look? Were you safe and happy? Were you finally enjoying the good life you deserve? Was it easy for you to imagine a job you enjoy where your coworkers respect you? Were you able to imagine an intact, secure family free from abuse?

When you visualized yourself in the future, did you have an image of how you might look? Imagine looking at yourself, completely naked, in a full-length mirror. What do you see? Look at your hair, your face, your neck, shoulders, arms, hands, body, and feet. Do parts of your body make you feel uncomfortable or embarrassed when you imagine them? Do individual features look "ugly" to you? Are these the same parts your ex-abuser told you were ugly?

Your abuser probably focused some of his humiliating comments on your physical appearance. Many women in our culture are very vulnerable to criticism about their looks. If he said you were too skinny or too fat, too short or too tall, your breasts were too small or too large, or other physical criticisms, these beliefs may still be with you. The more criticisms of your body he leveled at you, the harder it is to let go of them.

Though you now understand that his criticisms were part of the abuse, they still may affect your self-concept. You can know, intellectually, that his comments were designed to humiliate and control you. Nevertheless, dismissing them on an emotional level is difficult. It may take a long time to believe that your beauty does not, by any means, depend on the judgments of a cruel, controlling, abusive man.

Post Traumatic Stress Disorder (Revisited)

If your abuse was particularly severe, you may be suffering to some degree from post traumatic stress disorder, or PTSD (see chapter 7, "When Feelings Overwhelm You"). Several emotional factors may suggest the presence of PTSD. Do you find the memory of the abuse (physical, sexual, or emotional) suddenly consumes your thinking for seemingly no reason? This phenomenon, called *intrusive recall*, can interfere in very debilitating ways with your daily life. At times, you may feel you are having a flashback and are reliving a particularly traumatic event. At other times, you may feel as though you are having a particularly strong, almost physical recall of the abuse.

A common symptom of PTSD is *hypervigilance*. Hypervigilance is the feeling that you are always on your guard and can never relax. If you jump out of your skin when someone touches you from behind or at sudden loud noises, you are not completely beyond the effects of the abuse. These powerful mental and physical "memories" show that more work is needed to get beyond the trauma you experienced.

Another symptom that could suggest PTSD is *dissociation*. Dissociation is the perception that you are outside your body. If your relationship was especially violent, you may have found that during an attack, you felt as if you left your physical body and were observing the beating from above, looking down on it. This ability to escape the trauma of physical abuse helped you to survive the horrors of the relationship.

All of us experience a very mild form of dissociation every now and then. A good example of this occurs when you are driving along a highway and suddenly you realize you don't remember the last 5 miles. At first it may scare you, but then you realize you were daydreaming but your driving was just fine. These sorts of experiences are not caused by trauma but are the result of stress or distraction.

The form of dissociation that occurs after a traumatic event is similar to daydreams but much more intense. Now that you are out of the abusive relationship, you may find that you dissociate in frightening ways. You may experience episodes in which you completely lose a block of time. You may have experienced periods when minutes, hours, or even days had passed, but you couldn't remember them. It is often difficult for your mind and body to let go of defense mechanisms you used for survival. If you find you are experiencing episodes of dissociation that are interfering with your daily life, this is a clear sign of more healing to do.

On the other hand, do you find that you push any thoughts of the abuse out of your mind? Are you unable to think at all about that horrible time? Do your friends and family know that the topic of the abuse is off-limits? If someone asks you about it, do you immediately turn the conversation away from that subject? Do you try everything you can think of to wipe the abuse out of your memory? If you are engaging in *avoidant thinking*, it is because those thoughts are too painful even to allow them into your conscious mind. Until you can come to terms with the abuse, think about it, analyze it, and move past it, the pain is unlikely to go away. Avoidant thinking is another sign that you are not yet healed.

Behavioral Signs: Connections with Others

One way to assess your healing progress is to examine your daily activities. Often, if you are not able to detect the psychological pain that indicates a need for healing, you might be able to see the behavioral signs.

Now that you are out of the abusive relationship, how are your interactions with others? Have you been able to maintain some of your old friendships or establish new bonds with others? Do you feel that you have an effective support system of people you love and who love you in return?

How are your relationships with those who were there for you during and immediately after the abuse, those with whom you feel safe now? Are you able to let go of your sense of embarrassment, anger, and guilt in order to stay connected to them? Can you look them in the eyes and feel like an equal, or do you continue to feel indebted to them in a way that makes you feel small? If you do not feel strong and equal to your friends, this indicates additional healing is needed.

What about those who were not "there for you" during the abuse, those who abandoned you. Have you decided where they fit into your life now? It's all up to you. You may decide that some of them should not be in your life anymore. Perhaps others are important to you and you can keep them in your life despite their inability to support you during the abuse (see chapter 11, "The Reactions of Others"). Do you feel comfortable with the roles these people have in your life now? If not, you may still be struggling with healing.

Now consider the new people in your life. Do you worry that they will hurt you in some way? Do you feel inferior around them because you were in an abusive relationship? Whenever there's the smallest glitch in your friendship, do you panic and go overboard trying to make it OK again? Do you fear that these new friends might not be there for you when you need them?

These doubts and insecurities are perfectly normal in light of the abuse you suffered. It's hard to trust anyone again, but you need a support network of friends and family. If your answers to the questions in this section demonstrate your ongoing distrust and fear of getting close, this is a further sign that there is still work to be done.

Taking Care of Yourself

In the time following the abusive relationship, how well have you taken care of yourself? Are you being good to yourself? Are you treating yourself well? Or are you focusing most of your caring energy on others? If you look at your life objectively, does it seem as though you are doing more for others than you are for yourself? Do you go out of your way to assist and tend to others who are having a difficult time? What about when you are the one having a rough time? Are you able to care for yourself as well as you care for them?

Immersing yourself in the problems of others may be a way of hiding from yourself, of avoiding the pain and discomfort of working through *your* trauma. If you can spend all your time thinking of others, you don't have to think about yourself. What it really means is that you are still not ready to deal with your own pain, and dealing with that is key to healing.

Taking Care of Your Physical Health

Your emotional well-being and your physical health are closely linked. How well are you taking care of your body? Do you listen when your body informs you that you are tired and run down? If you get sick, do you allow yourself to relax and get well or do you force yourself to go on, no matter what? Is it difficult for you to let others take care of you? Think back to a time when you were ill before the abuse. Were you this hard on yourself back then? If not, your refusal to give your body a break now may be related to the aftereffect of the abuse. It may be a way of denying weakness or even punishing yourself. Whatever the exact connection, it is a further sign there is still work that you need to do to overcome the effects of that relationship.

Earlier in this chapter, you read about imagining your body 5 years into the future. Dealing with food may continue to be a problem for you if your abuser destroyed your body image. If you severely restrict your food intake, diet excessively, exercise compulsively, eat in binges, or are caught up in binge-and-purge cycles, you need to focus your healing efforts on these dangerous and self-destructive behaviors (see chapter 13, "Beginning to Heal").

If you are using alcohol or other drugs to escape from your frightening emotions and memories, this is a clear sign you are still suffering the effects of the abuse. Compare your drug use now with your use before the abusive relationship. If you are using more alcohol or other drugs, using different or stronger drugs, or getting high more often than you did before, this is a strong indication of the continuing presence of the abuse in your life. Abusing these substances will delay healing and prevent you from regaining your life. Your abuser doesn't deserve to continue having this much power over you. You may feel you had a problem with alcohol or other drugs before the relationship and still have a problem. If you feel your substance use is out of your control, many resources are available to help you overcome your addictions and continue down the path of healing (see "Resources" at the end of this book).

Some survivors of abusive and violent relationships have a tendency to engage in self-injurious behaviors. This was discussed in chapter 7, "When Feelings Overwhelm You," but it is important enough to mention again here. Have you cut, burned, or physically hurt yourself in other ways? Many survivors experience a sense of numbness that overwhelms them even after the relationship is over. Wounding themselves is a test to see if they can feel. For others, such injuries are signs of self-loathing or self-punishment that stem from extremely low levels of self-worth. If you are engaging in these abusive acts, you need to do more healing.

Help with Healing

The signs of unfinished healing discussed in this chapter are just some of the most common indications that you have work left to do. There are sure to be other signs as well. Recognizing that you are not fully recovered from the abuse is a healthy part of the healing process. The awareness allows you to continue to move toward becoming the person you want to be and having the fulfilling life you desire.

Keep in mind that if you find this process too difficult to do on your own, you might want to consider getting some help. As we have mentioned before, getting help does not mean that you are weak or that there is something wrong with you. It means that you have the courage and strength to reclaim your life after an abusive relationship (see chapter 13, "Beginning to Heal").

Is the Negative Talk Yours?

Hearing your abuser's critical, belittling comments in your memory is very different from telling yourself the same things. The transition from his voice to yours may have happened without your even realizing it. To assess where the negative talk is coming from now, fill out the worksheet below.

For 1 week, write down the most common negative remarks you "hear" in your mind each day. Make a note each time you catch yourself thinking something negative about you. Then, at the end of each day, record them on the following list. Next to each comment write whose "voice" it was you were hearing, his or yours or someone else's.

Sunday

Remark _____

_____

Whose voice? _____

Monday

Remark _____

_____

Whose voice? _____

Tuesday

Remark _____

_____

Whose voice? _____

Wednesday

Remark _____

_____

Whose voice? _____

Thursday

Remark _____

_____

Whose voice? _____

Friday

Remark _____

_____

Whose voice? _____

Saturday

Remark _____

_____

Whose voice? _____

Note: As you do this exercise, you may find that the voice you hear is someone else's: a parent, someone who abused you in childhood, a teacher, or other significant person in your life. Those voices should also be considered in your healing process (see chapter 13, "Beginning to Heal").

After 1 month has gone by, try repeating this exercise. By comparing your answers you will be able to see what changes there have been in your self-talk.

Is the Negative Talk Yours? (II) 1 month later

Sunday

Remark _____

_____

Whose voice? _____

Monday

Remark _____

_____

Whose voice? _____

Tuesday

Remark _____

_____

Whose voice? _____

Wednesday

Remark _____

_____

Whose voice? _____

Thursday

Remark _____

_____

Whose voice? _____

Friday

Remark ——————————————————————————

———————————————————————————————

Whose voice? ————————————————————————

Saturday

Remark ——————————————————————————

———————————————————————————————

Whose voice? ————————————————————————

Managing Your Stress

I feel strung so tight the slightest problem will make me snap.

EVELYN, AGE 73

I haven't slept well in weeks. Whenever I close my eyes, a million thoughts keep whirling through my mind. I try to ignore them, but they won't go away.

CARA, AGE 38

I know I did the right thing by getting out but it feels like too much to handle right now. I can't study, I can't concentrate in class, and I just flunked a big exam.

DI, AGE 21

Myth: Just the process of working through problems helps you feel peaceful and more relaxed.

Myth: Feeling totally stressed out is a normal part of life. There really isn't much you can do to make it any better.

Myth: If you think and act in positive, healthy ways, you will automatically be less stressed.

*R*egaining your life after an abusive relationship can be very rewarding, but it is also an extremely stressful time. The myriad of emotions you are experiencing takes a toll on you, psychologically and physically. You *can* decrease your overall level of stress and make this difficult transition easier. This chapter is unique in that it consists mostly of a series of 10 self-exploration exercises designed to help reduce the effects of stress in your life. These exercises will follow a brief overview of the causes and effects of stress during this transitional period in your life.

The Effects of Stress

Stress affects each person in distinctive ways, emotionally and physically. Some people become anxious and on edge when under stress. Others become cranky and irritable. Still others become fatigued, angry, or withdrawn.

You may have been under such severe stress for so long during your relationship that your mind and body "think" it's normal. The time and effort required for you to "de-stress" following your relationship will depend on how abusive it was and how much time has passed. Although your life is better now than when you were with him, it may not be free from the stress linked to the abuse.

Obviously, you are experiencing the emotional stress that comes with working through the aftereffect of the abuse. If safety is still a concern for you, that alone creates tremendous stress. After any relationship, a new daily life must be established. This new life comes with many changes. Even when those changes are good, they can still produce stress. Routine tasks such as setting up a new home, reestablishing your financial security, finding work, or getting your children settled into a new routine can place a great strain on you.

It's important to consider just how and to what extent this stress is affecting your daily functioning. Is it reducing your ability to think clearly and make sound decisions? Is it creating feelings and moods that are pushing people away and isolating you? Is it altering your behavior so that you are not accomplishing your goals and living an effective life? The keys to healing are being aware of the stress you are experiencing and finding new ways to reduce or cope with it.

Stress and the Self

One way stress takes its toll is by chipping away at your self-esteem. Are you much more critical of yourself when you make a mistake than you used to be? Are you quick to assume simple tasks are too overwhelming even to attempt? If you attempt a task, do you suspect your efforts won't be "good enough"? Is it difficult to concentrate and stay focused on the task at hand?

When you think back on your life, are you intensely critical of the path you've taken, the choices you've made? Do you look at your life and tell yourself that you've really screwed it up and you'll never amount to much? Thoughts such as these are ways ongoing stress diminishes your view of yourself and your abilities. As you identify the stress in your life and begin to deal with it, you will become more effective in accomplishing your goals. Self-esteem issues are discussed in greater detail in chapter 14, "Believing in Yourself."

Stress and Your Relationships

One of the most effective coping mechanisms is the presence of people in your life who support you, are there for you, and offer unconditional love. If you lost many of these social supports during the course of the abusive relationship, it may take time to rebuild such a network. A responsive and caring ear when you need to talk can do wonders for reducing your stress. If you are finding it difficult to make new friends, consider joining a local group or organization in which you can meet new people. Make an effort to revive old friendships that you feel can benefit you. See if lost friendships can be repaired (refer to chapter 11, "The Reactions of Others," for more discussion of friendships during and after an abusive relationship). Nearly all stressful situations are more difficult if you feel you must deal with them without the support of others.

Stress and Your Body

What is all this stress doing to your body? Have you been more prone to headaches than usual? Are the muscles in your neck and back tight and sore? Do you often experience "butterflies" in your stomach or suffer from frequent stomachaches, diarrhea, constipation, or cramping?

Stress affects your body in many ways. If you have noticed that you are suffering from one or more undiagnosed physical complaints, they may stem from the stress you are confronting. It's important for your emotional and physical health to find effective strategies for reducing your levels of stress.

Letting Go

It's important to decide to let go of your expectations about how your life "should" be. As we've said often, the abuse wasn't your fault and neither is your current process of starting over. You need to stop judging your feelings and reactions. Despite whether a particular emotion is small or large, easy or difficult, if it feels stressful, it's stressful. After hiding your feelings for so long, releasing them now is bound to create stress.

It doesn't matter what anyone else thinks about your life. What does matter is that you do what you need to do to be happy and fulfilled. If this means taking the time and energy to care for yourself, then that is what you need to do.

Whatever the sources of your stress, there are ways to help reduce their negative effects. Learning effective strategies to cope with this emotional stress will allow you to continue your work toward a healthy life. Take the time to discover which of the following techniques works the best for you. Reducing your stress is just as important as all those other "to-dos" on your list!

Take Care of Yourself

Taking care of *you* may not be such an easy task after an abusive relationship. Did your ex-partner make you feel that your problems, concerns, and pain were trivial and insignificant? Were you unable to receive his support when you needed it? Did he instill the idea that you were selfish to be concerned with your problems? Now, after months or years of your needs being ignored, it may take time to learn how to be good to yourself.

Being good to yourself is not being self-centered. It means treating yourself as well as you treat others. If this is difficult for you, then you will need to go slowly.

Start by making a list of little personal luxuries you never seem to find the time to do. These special pleasures can be as simple as reading a magazine, sitting down to watch TV for an hour or two, going for a walk, or taking a long, hot bath. Put your list where you will see it frequently. Indulge in at least one item on your list each day. If you can't find the time for them, see if there is any way to reduce your workload, ask a friend to help out, or, if possible, pay someone to do your least-favorite chore. Try to devote at least 1 hour per day completely to treating yourself. If you just can't seem to find that hour, start with 15 minutes and increase it a little each week until you can squeeze out an hour or more each day. You will feel the stress-reducing effects of this daily "special time" throughout the remainder of your day and night.

SELF-EXPLORATION: Exercise 2
Schedule Stressful Thoughts

What do you do when you are obsessing over stressful concerns? Do you try to push them out of your mind? You know the more you try to force those worries out of your head, the more difficult it becomes to concentrate on anything else, such as your work. One way you can go easier on yourself is to put your worry on a schedule. Allow yourself a limited amount of time several times each day to focus on what is bothering you. This is called *thought partitioning*. Here's how to do it.

For 1 week, write down all (or most) of your stressful and negative thoughts. Don't censor your thoughts or make them sound less stressful than they are—just write them down. No one will ever see them but you. After a week, review your negative thoughts. If you are like most people, you'll see a pattern of the same or similar themes appearing over and over.

When you feel your negative thought patterns creeping into your mind, establish a specified, limited time for fretting. Tell yourself if you work for, say, 45 minutes, you will then allow yourself 10 minutes to sit and worry about whatever's on your mind. At first, you may have to work for shorter periods before your "worry break," such as 15 minutes or half an hour. Eventually, you should be able to increase that to a couple of hours or more during which you are free from those nagging thoughts. After some practice with partitioning, you will be able to say to your stressful thoughts, "Not now, I'll get to you later."

SELF-EXPLORATION: Exercise 2a
Week One: Stressful Thoughts Inventory

Sunday _____

_____

_____

_____

Monday _____

_____

_____

_____

Tuesday _____

_____

_____

_____

Wednesday _____

_____

_____

_____

Thursday _____

_____

_____

_____

_____

Friday _____

_____

_____

_____

Saturday _____

_____

_____

_____

Week Two: Thought Partitioning Assessment

Now, record the average amount of time in between "worry breaks." Document each day. Don't be concerned if initially you go for only an hour or less between breaks. You should notice an increase in the length of time between worry breaks as the week or weeks continue.

Day of the week   *Average length of time between worry breaks*

Sunday   _____

Monday   _____

Tuesday   _____

Wednesday   _____

Thursday   _____

Friday   _____

Saturday   _____

Thought Stopping

Besides scheduling time for stressful thoughts, you can also work on stopping them. You may feel as though thoughts enter and exit your brain whenever they want, but the truth is you can control much of your thinking. Look at your list of negative thoughts from the previous exercise. Did you find that many of them were self-judgmental? Were they saying that you are inadequate or unable to succeed or that negative events are always going to be a part of your life? Chances are, on an intellectual level, you know these thoughts are not really true, but, nevertheless, there they are.

If you have numerous and frequent unrealistic thoughts, you may benefit from a therapeutic technique called *thought stopping*. Thought stopping is designed to weed out negative, unproductive, and ineffective thoughts, allowing you to think more positively about yourself and your life.

The first step in thought stopping is to recognize the negative and unrealistic thoughts you are having. You began this recognition by writing down your thoughts for a week (exercise 2a). If you completed the exercise in 2a, you already have your list. Circle all of the thoughts that are self-defeating and unrealistic. Such thoughts might include berating yourself for failing to finish a project, worrying endlessly about a situation you can't control, or obsessing about a past event that still upsets you.

The next step is breaking the cycle of unwanted thoughts and stopping them in their tracks. You do this by performing specific physical actions at the moment one of the thoughts begins. These actions are designed to redirect your thoughts abruptly and completely. For example, the next time you realize you are having one of your unwanted thoughts yell, "Stop!" and forcefully stomp your foot.

Of course, people are going be startled or think you are rather strange if you do this in public. So another technique is to place a rubber band around your wrist. When you are in public and the thoughts begin, snap the rubber band just hard enough to notice (but not hard enough to leave a mark). This sharp interruption will temporarily stop the thought. If the same thoughts come back a few minutes later, snap your wrist again. If they continue to intrude, that's OK for now. This process won't eliminate your ingrained thinking patterns immediately. Spend a week recognizing your unwanted thoughts and trying to stop them.

Thought Substititution

The next step is to substitute thoughts that are more realistic, encouraging, and positive. This is called *reframing*. For a week, try substituting the new thoughts each time you stop one of the old ones.

Thought stopping and substitution will not change your self-defeating thoughts overnight. It takes work and time. If you follow the procedures and practice substituting new, positive beliefs, those unwanted thoughts will begin to decrease and possibly disappear altogether. You also need to remember that this process is not intended to be used to hide or mask your true feelings about the abuse or your current life. It should be used only to stop your out-of-control, unproductive negative thoughts that are disrupting your life on a routine basis.

In the column on the left, write the old unproductive thoughts from your list in exercise 3a. Next, in the right-hand column, write substitute positive thoughts you will put in place of those old thoughts.

	Old negative thought	*New positive thought*
Sunday	_____	_____
	_____	_____
	_____	_____
Monday	_____	_____
	_____	_____
	_____	_____

Tuesday _____   _____

_____   _____

_____   _____

Wednesday _____   _____

_____   _____

_____   _____

Thursday _____   _____

_____   _____

_____   _____

Friday _____   _____

_____   _____

_____   _____

Saturday _____   _____

_____   _____

_____   _____

Sunday _____   _____

_____   _____

_____   _____

Now that you have finished your lists, put your new thoughts into action. Whenever you find one of those old thoughts creeping into your mind, immediately substitute your new, self-affirming thought. In time, these new thoughts should emerge without prompting and the negative thoughts will diminish and possibly disappear.

There's Always Too Much to Do

Do you feel you have so many projects on your plate that accomplishing them seems utterly hopeless? One possible solution to this source of stress is to organize your life so that you will use your time as effectively as possible. One way to do this is to *prioritize*. When the mental to-do list becomes too long, stop, sit down in some quiet place, and list everything you need to do. Don't worry for now about how long the list gets or what's important and what isn't. Just get everything on there.

Next, begin to break that master list down into smaller, more manageable segments. Create a to-do list for just this morning, this afternoon, before the end of the day, this week, by the end of the month, and long-term goals farther into the future. Look through that list and decide which items are *realistic* short-term goals. Be reasonable. Don't put more on your short-term list than you can actually accomplish. Set yourself up for success, not failure. Think how good it will feel to cross everything off today's list! Banish the tasks you know cannot be accomplished today or this week to the long-term list, and be sure to cross them off your immediate list (just doing *that* feels good!).

After you have completed your lists, review each again to be sure it is reasonable given the amount of time you have to accomplish the tasks. See if some tasks can be removed completely. Again, why set yourself up to fail? Finally, prioritize the items in each list.

If you cannot accomplish an entire goal, set it up so you can accomplish a part of it. For example, if a goal is a big and complex one, such as finding a new job, you probably cannot complete it in a single day. So break it down into smaller subgoals, some for today, such as working on your résumé, writing a cover letter, or beginning to go through the classified ads in the newspaper. A longer-range goal for the week might be to complete and polish your résumé, get copies made, and apply for one job. Next week, a reasonable goal might be to apply for three additional jobs.

If your to-do list says "find a job," it feels overwhelming, impossible, and very stressful. By giving yourself smaller, reachable goals, you will feel less stressed and much more accomplished as you cross off each step along the way.

Deep Breathing

Note: If you have been experiencing any form of dissociation as discussed in Chapter 8, "Signs of Unfinished Healing," you may want to avoid the following relaxation techniques. These exercises involve various forms of visualization or meditation, which have been shown to trigger dissociative reactions in some individuals.

One of the most basic techniques in stress management involves altering your breathing pattern. When you become stressed, you breathe faster and shallower. If you are experiencing a lot of stress or are feeling especially anxious, try modifying your breathing using the following technique.

First, put one hand on your chest and the other hand on your abdomen just below your rib cage. As you breathe, notice which hand is moving. If it's the hand on your chest, your breathing is too shallow.

With your hands still in place, breathe in deeply and slowly for a count of five and then exhale slowly, again for a count of five. If you didn't feel your hand on your stomach move, try breathing deeply and slowly again, this time attempting to bring the air all the way down into your diaphragm. If you do this correctly, the hand on your abdomen area should move along with each breath. When you succeed in breathing from your diaphragm, take five deep breaths, breathing in and out to a count of five for each inhale and each exhale.

Deep breathing relaxes you and may help slow some of your "runaway" thoughts. If you are under a great deal of stress, performing this deep-breathing exercise on a routine basis several times a day may be helpful.

Become aware of specific settings or situations that create stress in you such as sitting in traffic, a ringing telephone, arriving at your job, going to class. Mark those places in some way to remind yourself to breathe deeply. One easy way to do this is to place some sort of sticker in each stressful location where you will see it easily. The sticker doesn't have to say anything in particular as long as seeing it reminds you to breathe. For example, if answering the phone at work increases your stress, put a sticker on the phone to remind yourself to take a deep breath or two before you pick up the receiver. If you find that you get stressed while driving, put a sticker on the dashboard. Any place that triggers a stress response is a good place for a sticker.

Progressive Muscle Relaxation

Progressive muscle relaxation (PMR) is a proven technique for reducing tension in your body. PMR involves tensing and relaxing muscle groups throughout your body, one group at a time. It can be particularly helpful if you store stress in your body. It is also especially helpful when you are having difficulty falling asleep at night.

Here's an effective PMR exercise. It's best if you can listen to the instructions while you are relaxing, so you might want to record this or have a friend read it to you.

Sit in a comfortable chair or lie on the floor or a bed. Begin the process by tensing your right foot and holding that tension for a slow count of five. Then release the tension in your foot and completely relax it for another count of five. Next, tense the muscles of your right ankle for a count of five and relax them for a count of five. Now tense, then release, your right calf muscles in the same way. After you finish tensing and relaxing all the muscles in your right leg, move on to your left foot and leg. Slowly continue this progressive tensing and releasing of individual muscle groups until you have covered your entire body from your toes to your scalp. The chart below will guide you through all your muscle groups in the recommended sequence.

Progressive Muscle Relaxation Muscle Groups

Be sure to include all of the following areas when performing PMR techniques. For each muscle group, remember to tense and relax for a count of five each.

> Right foot
> Right ankle
> Right calf
> Right thigh
> Left foot
> Left ankle

Left calf
Left thigh
Buttocks
Back
Stomach
Chest
Right hand
Right wrist
Right forearm
Right bicep
Left hand
Left wrist
Left forearm
Left bicep
Shoulders
Neck
Face
Jaw
Tongue
Forehead
Scalp

Be sure to include every muscle group. Do not rush through the process by tightening your entire leg or arm. Take each individual part separately. For example, tense and release your hand, then your wrist, then your forearm, and then your bicep.

Try PMR for a few weeks. As with all relaxation techniques, it might take a while to learn to relax completely. If unwanted thoughts enter your mind as you are going through the process, gently push them out and focus on your body. Do not become angry or upset if you lose your focus. It takes time, but once you are skilled at PMR, it can be a great weapon against stress.

Visualization

Visualization is another method of de-stressing you may find helpful. Visualization involves creating a relaxing image in your mind that helps you to focus on something other than the stress. An effective visualization not only transports you psychologically to a more relaxing place, but it also helps expel unwanted thoughts. The more you practice visualizations, the more effective they will become.

A good way to introduce yourself to visualization is to use an established pattern of images. As you become more accustomed to this relaxation technique, you may want to create your own visualizations.

Try using the following visualization to guide you through a relaxing thought process. If you find that you need to hear it rather than just reading it, you can record it. This exercise usually takes between 10 and 20 minutes. The visualization should help you escape your stressful world. If it reduces your stress, you can imagine it anytime you want or use it as a model for creating your own, personal visualization (see Exercise 9).

Finding Your Place[1]

Find a comfortable position. Allow your eyes to close. Take a moment to focus your attention on your breathing. You are breathing in and breathing out, breathing in and breathing out.

Imagine yourself taking a paintbrush and painting a big blue screen across your field of vision. Now dip the paintbrush in the white paint and add fluffy white clouds to your sky. As you set down your paintbrush you are drawn into the scene. You step through the picture onto a fluffy cloud. The cloud takes you safely on a journey.

---

[1]Adapted from "Finding Your Place," by Heather Oberheim. Used by permission.

Allow yourself to float on the soft, fluffy cloud. You can jump onto another cloud or just rest on your own cloud. As you are floating in the sky, take a moment to look down at the scenes below. Your cloud is perfectly safe. You float, watching calm and peaceful scenes pass below. Find a place below that feels especially safe and serene. Allow yourself to look at this place as your cloud stops above it. Slowly, your cloud floats you down to this place. You step off the cloud to explore.

Explore this new world. Allow your senses to awaken. Listen to the sounds in this place. Pay attention to how you feel here. Permit your body to absorb your surroundings totally through all of your senses. There's no hurry; take your time.

As you look around and sense this place, see if you can find something—an object, a thought, or a vision—you can take with you that makes you feel tranquil and protected. Go over to it and touch it, see it, hear it, and smell it. Allow all of your senses to hold this thing you have found.

Take a moment to breathe in this place one last time, absorbing all that you can. This is *your* place. Take your new, special possession and slowly step back onto the cloud as it floats up into the sky. Give yourself time to say goodbye. Watch your place fade away into the distance.

The soft fluffy cloud floats through the sky and you float away with it. In the distance you see the blue screen you painted. The cloud floats toward the screen. Take a step through the screen and watch your cloud float away. Take out your new belonging from your special place. Hold it for a moment. Put it away in a place where you can picture it easily whenever you want.

Now, allow your body to feel the real world beneath it. Focus on the parts of your body that are touching the floor or chair and the parts touching the air. Bring your attention back to your body and your surroundings. Allow your fingers and toes to wiggle. Slowly, very slowly, open your eyes. Give yourself time to stretch and awaken your body from your journey.

Meditation

Meditation is another effective form of stress reduction. Meditation techniques may be divided into two basic categories. One involves becoming more in touch with your thoughts and feelings, while the other uses a mantra or chant to focus your mind *away* from your stressful thoughts.

If you are interested in learning more about meditation, you will find many good books on the subject, and most communities have meditation centers. To experience the flavor of this relaxation technique, try the following brief and simple meditation exercise.

Meditation Exercise

Find a comfortable place to sit. Make sure your feet are on the floor and you are sitting upright. Close your eyes and take a deep breath. Pay attention to your breathing. If you are not breathing from your diaphragm, shift your breathing so you can feel your stomach rising and falling with each breath.

Each time you inhale, say to yourself, "Relaxation in." As you exhale say to yourself, "Tension out." Repeat these words to yourself throughout the exercise. Clear your mind of all other thoughts. This "chanting," or mantra, will help you focus your thoughts away from your stress and anxiety. Do not worry when these thoughts return, just gently push them out of your mind.

Continue meditating for approximately 15 to 30 minutes. When you decide that it is time to end, slowly open your eyes. Gently move your arms, legs, and body. When you feel ready, continue with your day. It's best if you can find a time to meditate at least once each day.

Create Your Personal Relaxation Tape

If you have found that a certain combination of methods works well for you, for example, peaceful music and visualization, you may want to create your own relaxation tape. It's not as difficult as you may think. Design a visualization that works well for you. Include in it a scene or place that you find particularly relaxing. Describe any details you find soothing and comforting, including sounds, sights, smells, tastes, and sensations of touch.

You can combine many of the techniques discussed in this chapter (PMR, visualization, breathing techniques) with relaxing music or sounds to make your own personalized tape. If you do not feel comfortable recording the tape yourself, ask a friend to help. Record it in a place where there will be no distractions and no unwanted noise. In the background, play those sounds or music selections that trigger relaxation in you. You can keep your tape with you wherever you go and listen whenever you need to.

Physical Exercise

An often overlooked form of relaxation is physical exercise. It's amazing how a brisk walk, stretching, aerobics, weight lifting, swimming, sports, or other forms of working out can help to de-stress you. If you have exercised regularly in the past, but have not been doing so recently, now is the time to start up again. A good workout at least three times a week will help reduce your overall stress level and decrease the negative effects of the stress.

Many people find yoga to be a particularly restful, yet powerful form of exercise. Yoga not only exercises your body and stretches your muscles, but also can focus on areas of your body in which you store your stress. Yoga exercises can be done that will address specific stress-related areas: your neck, shoulders, back, or abdomen.

10

What About the Children?

He was never violent with the children. They loved their father. I didn't want the children to grow up without a father.

NAOMI, AGE 28

The main reason I stayed so long was, I thought I might never see my kids again. I was afraid he would find a way to make me the villain.

VICKI, AGE 24

When he hit my oldest daughter, I felt I had to stay to protect my children. I had no choice.

SUSAN, AGE 35

Myth: An abusive father is better than no father at all.

Myth: Abusers rarely target the children.

Myth: If children never witness the actual abuse, they are not damaged by it.

*T*his chapter is for those of you who have children who experienced the nightmare of abuse. Sadly, many abusive relationships include children in various family configurations. No matter how your children are related to your former abuser, they may be suffering the consequences of his actions. Witnessing relationship abuse and violence can have devastating effects on children.

The majority of men who abuse their female partners also abuse their children. Approximately one in four incidents of relationship abuse involves injury to children. No matter whether the children are directly abused themselves, they often witness the battering and mistreatment of their mother.

Your children need not have been the direct recipients of abuse or violence to suffer profound psychological and emotional effects. All children who live in homes where domestic violence occurs are victims. Witnessing their mother being victimized by their father was terribly frightening and confusing for your children. Observing such behavior from a man who was not their father carries with it different but equally terrifying reactions.

This chapter is for those of you who brought your children out of the violent relationship with you. It will focus on the aftereffects of the abusive relationship on your children, how to protect them from your abuser, and what you can do to help them to recover and heal along with you.

The Children's Experience of the Abuse

First, even if you tried to hide or camouflage the abuse from your kids, you should assume they knew about it. Your children probably lived in fear and confusion. They were afraid of being abused themselves; they were afraid for you; and they were afraid of losing the people they depended on to care for them. They were confused because their environment was unpredictable as a result of the recurring cycle of abuse discussed in chapter 1, "Were You in an Abusive Relationship?" Their life felt safe and secure at times, but then the abuse and terror would begin again, throwing all they knew into chaos. Safety and consistency are two necessary conditions for children to grow up psychologically and emotionally healthy. Despite your best efforts, you were not able to provide these circumstances for your children. While your children were enduring the abusive relationship, they had neither safety nor consistency.

Your children may have found themselves in a situation where they could never be sure from one day to the next if they had a parent who would be able to be there for them. They certainly could not trust the abuser, and, often, you were so physically and emotionally traumatized, they were reluctant to ask for what few resources you had left. Just as you never felt safe, your children probably didn't either.

This was not your fault. You had little control over your life then. Throughout this book, we have often discussed your need to do whatever was necessary to survive. Chances are you were also doing what was necessary to ensure the survival of your children. Survival had to take priority over perfect parenting. Remember, you got your kids out of a dangerous situation; *you rescued them.* As you discover your path toward healing, you will usually find that your children will recover along with you.

While the reactions of children who witness relationship abuse and domestic violence vary from child to child, there are some categories of responses that are fairly typical. Your ability to recognize in your children the psychological, emotional, and behavioral effects of the abuse will assist you in guiding them through their healing process.

Psychological and Emotional Reactions

Children's psychological and emotional reactions will vary extensively depending on the nature of the abuse, their overall adjustment prior to the abuse, and their individual personality characteristics. Because the symptoms discussed here occur more frequently in children who witness abuse or are victims themselves, keeping a close eye on your children will help you detect if some of these signs are present. However, it's also important to remember that many children with *no* history of abuse may exhibit some of these characteristics as they grow and develop. Therefore, while you should not overlook any signs of psychological and emotional difficulties, they may not stem directly from the abuse.

Low self-esteem is perhaps the most common characteristic to watch for in your children. This is probably the most pervasive and debilitating of all the psychological effects. As we discussed earlier, your children may feel at fault for the abuse and guilty for being unable to stop it. They view themselves as failures. This poor self-image has the potential to affect nearly everything they attempt in school, sports, personal goals, and relationships with others.

Your children may exhibit *physical and intellectual problems.* For instance, children of abused mothers often show delays in thinking, verbal, and motor skills development. They often experience sleep disorders (which may or may not be associated with depression), stuttering, and psychosomatic illnesses (illnesses that have no physical cause, such as frequent stomachaches). In addition, they tend to be much more impulsive than average, engaging in inappropriate behaviors without regard for potential negative consequences.

Your children may experience many of the same strong emotions you felt during and in the aftermath of your abusive relationship. Probably the most common, and entirely normal, emotional responses in children are *anxiety* and *depression.* Your children, to an even greater extent than yourself, may perceive the abuse to have been completely beyond their control.

Even if you are in a situation now where you know your children are out of danger, *they* may not feel safe. They may be too young to understand all of the precautions you have taken to ensure their safety. They observed that you were unable to protect yourself and possibly them from the violence in the past. Consequently, they may continue to be afraid not only for themselves but also for you. They know they were unable to stop the abuse in the past, so they feel they would be powerless to prevent or stop it now. How could such a looming threat *not* produce severe anxiety?

While you have reduced or eliminated contact with your abuser, the children may still be interacting with him through court-ordered visitation or joint custody (this will be discussed in greater detail later). Although safeguards may be in place to prevent any further obvious abuse from occurring during the children's visits with your abuser, understanding and feeling confident of that may be difficult for them. So it's possible that your children may feel even greater anxiety than you.

Your children's perception of powerlessness over bad events in their lives may lead to serious depression. The symptoms of depression in children are similar to those in adults. They include social withdrawal, frequent and easily provoked crying, a lack of enthusiasm in fun activities, lack of energy, changes in sleeping and eating habits, and, sometimes, suicidal thoughts.

Self-blame is another strong emotion your children may express following the abusive relationship. Your kids love their parents unconditionally; they may even express love for their father even though he was violent. They desperately want their parents to be happy, to get along, not to hurt each other, and to love them back. Your children may blame themselves for the abuse and for the failure of the relationship. They may see the violence as somehow their fault: that if they had behaved differently or better it would never have happened and you would all still be together.

Usually related to this self-blame is *intense guilt*. If you have older children they might feel they should have done something to intervene, to stop the abuse, to prevent you from being hurt. When older children (especially boys) try to step in, the results can be catastrophic. The child can be seriously injured or killed, or, in some cases, the child kills his or her mother's attacker. Most children, however, are too afraid and feel far too helpless to attempt to intervene. They have no choice but to live with the fear and terror of the abuse. Once they and their mother are safely away from the abuse, these children will often feel it was all their fault. If your children tried to intervene, they risked serious emotional and physical consequences for them and for you. If they tried but were unable to help, the guilt they are feeling may be overwhelming.

From a relatively safe vantage point in the aftermath of their mother's abuse, another emotion often emerges in children, as it may have in you: *anger*. As your children witnessed the abuse and violence, it was probably very clear that expressions of anger at that time were out of the question. They knew it would be dangerous and might make the abuse worse or turn it against them.

Now that you and they are out, the anger can awaken. It might be expressed as rage toward the abuser for his violent acts, outrage toward you for, in the child's mind, allowing the abuse to happen, or hostility toward themselves for causing or not preventing it. Children may engage in abusive acts toward you, siblings, peers, or women in general, modeled after the behaviors they witnessed in your abuser.

Finally, your children may suffer a *fear of abandonment*. They experienced helplessness and the terrifying feeling that neither parent would be there for them. Although their safety now depends upon being away from your abuser, they may feel abandoned by him nonetheless.

So many uncontrollable and horrible events have occurred in their life, how can they be sure the one parent they have, you, won't go away too? Eventually, over time, they will regain the trust and faith that you will be there for them, but fearing abandonment now, and perhaps for a while, is normal and, from their perspective, justified.

Behavioral Difficulties

If your children are unable to work out their psychological problems verbally, you might find they engage in extreme and inappropriate behavior patterns. This is called "acting out." All children will act out on occasion when angry or frustrated, but the behaviors mentioned here tend to be more common in children who have witnessed or experienced domestic abuse. These behaviors depend on the age of the child but may include frequent tantrums, greater-than-normal sibling aggression, running away from home, self-injurious behavior (head banging, cutting, burning, etc.), violent behavior toward pets or other animals, drug and alcohol abuse, and sexual impulsivity or promiscuity.

It would be a relief to know that any effects of the abuse would be evident immediately, so you could work to decrease them. Unfortunately, exposure to domestic violence may influence adjustment and behavior later in the child's life. For example, chil-

dren who witness abuse are, on average, less successful in establishing and maintaining their own relationships and marriages.
Moreover, experiencing violence as a child increases the tendency
for boys to engage in violence and creates a greater likelihood for
girls to become victims of violence as adults. It is not a forgone
conclusion that this will be true for your children. The safety, reassurance, and help you give your children now will significantly
reduce their risk for difficulties later.

Making It Better

Being a good parent is never easy. It may be even more difficult now,
as you are dealing with the stresses and strains of your own healing
process following the abuse. You know your kids are the most
important priority in your life, so you experience even more guilt
and more stress when you feel unable to give them the time and
energy they need from you. Some survivors find that at times they
displace the anger they feel toward their abuser onto their children.
You may have found yourself becoming angry more quickly with
your children, lashing out verbally when they misbehaved, or even
resorting to physical punishment you later regretted.

After what you've been through, and considering the energy you
need to expend on reclaiming your life, finding your emotions on a
short fuse at times is understandable. The same is true for your kids.
If you are seeing negative changes in your relationship with your
children, it is important to pay very close attention to how and when
your frustration with them builds toward an unwanted outburst.

When children are required to spend time with their father who
was also your abuser, they may find this confusing, uncomfortable,
and even frightening. They may express these feelings before or
after their visits as hostility toward you in the form of misbehav-
ior, ignoring your requests of them, or verbal displays of anger
directed at you.

So what can you do to help your children heal? Above all, try
not to take their acting out personally. It's not easy, but remember
that they may be directing some of these emotions toward you

because you are their only completely safe support. Afterward make sure you have a support of your own to talk with.

If your children are old enough to understand, explain to them that this is a difficult time, and everyone is on edge. Tell them that it's OK that you are all a little more touchy than usual. Let them know that eventually this will pass. Make sure that they know that you love them no matter what.

If you have more than one child, try to schedule one-on-one time with each of them. Often what one child needs to hear, say, or discuss is very different from another. Encourage them to talk about the abuse and about your abuser. As difficult as it may be, try to explain to them why things were and are the way they are without getting defensive. Help them to identify what it is they are feeling, and let them know that it's OK to feel that way. Often children may have difficulty identifying what it is they are feeling, and by acknowledging it and naming it (fear, anger, guilt) you are helping them to better understand themselves. Make sure they know they can always come to you to talk about anything. (See Talking to the Children later in this chapter for more detail.)

Talk to your children about violence. Without verbally attacking your abuser, since your children may still love him, talk about how no one should ever hurt anyone else. Explain what this means and how it affects the other person. They need to know not only that no one should ever abuse another but also that no one deserves to be abused. (See page 149 for further information.)

Allow them the time they need to heal. Since the abuse probably occurred during some critical developmental stages, you may find that some of their emotions or behaviors are a bit "younger" than those of other kids their age. This is natural given the circumstances. Remember the fear that you may have and may still live with. They also experienced this fear. Do whatever is necessary, within limits, to quell this fear. Allow them to sleep with a night light on or the door open. If they are truly fearful for themselves or for you, you may want to put a baby monitor in each room.

Give your children some extra loving. Increase the number of hugs and pats on the back. Spend a few extra minutes with them at bedtime. Try to offer some extra fun together time in a setting in which everyone feels good. This could be anything from going to the park for a picnic to watching a family video at home. Remind them of all their good qualities more frequently. These little gestures can go a long way toward reversing the effects of the strong negative emotions everyone is experiencing during this difficult time.

Develop some strategies to defuse an emotional situation before it gets out of control. These could include assigning each family member a code word or sentence that signals a 2-minute truce during which no one may speak (so everyone has the power to stop the escalation process). Trying to get all family members to talk about how they are feeling (using "I" statements) rather than what someone else said or did ("He said that . . ." "She just . . .") may help to keep arguments from getting as severe. Or you may want to have regular family meetings in which everyone is free to discuss anything without fear of punishment. These are just a few suggestions. It's usually best if you can develop your own interventions, maybe in consultation with your kids if they are old enough or with a therapist, if you have one, who is working with the children or with you.

Finally, get some time for yourself away from your children. This should be quality time; not when you are at work or when they are visiting your abuser and you are worrying about them. Try to set up a few hours each week when your kids can visit a friend's house or go to a trusted relative of yours. This will help prevent your frustration with them from building up to explosive levels.

Keep in mind, these strategies will probably not work every time. There are bound to be flare-ups, tantrums, and eruptions from time to time. But by thinking about what causes them and how to prevent or defuse them and by planning ahead, there's hope that the number and intensity can be minimized. If nothing helps, and your relationship with your kids continues to be difficult, some professional family counseling might be in order (this is further discussed later in this chapter).

Keeping Your Children Safe

All of the safety information discussed in chapter 2, "Are You Out of Danger Now?", pertains to the safety of your children as well. Beyond those important safeguards, the key to keeping your children safe is preventing access to them by your abuser.

If your abuser has no legal access, he may try to find illegal ways to see the children. His motive may be simply that, in his way, he loves and misses them. But more often, your former abuser will try to use the children to control and frighten *you*.

If you believe that your former partner may try to contact your children, it is important that you enlist the assistance and cooperation of everyone with whom the children spend time. All caretakers must be made aware of the possible danger. You should supply child care locations, schools, organized sports or other activity leaders, and baby-sitters with information, descriptions, and photos of your abuser and instruct them exactly to whom the child may be released. Today, most agencies with responsibilities for children are aware of these issues, but you should always double-check.

If your children are old enough to be without supervision at times, be sure they understand they must never allow your former abuser to contact or talk to them. Moreover, under no circumstances are they to go anywhere with him that has not been planned and approved by you. Explain to your children that though they may love their father and enjoy the time they spend with him, it's important to stick to planned visits so the good times never again have to become bad times.

Explain to your older children what they should do if he approaches them. Have safe houses of friends and relatives and other locations such as stores or offices where they can go if he approaches them when you are not home. Your children should understand they don't need to spend every minute being afraid, but they must grasp the potential danger and be prepared to act.

When Your Abuser Has Access to Your Children

Abusive men who are the biological or legal fathers of the children are more likely than normal fathers to fight for custody of their children in court following the breakup of a violent relationship. Not only is custody an opportunity for an abuser to exercise control, but he is also motivated by a desire to prove that the accusations of abuse are unfounded. Remember, most abusive men are experts at hiding their violent nature and can appear very loving and victimized.

Even worse, your abuser may use your children as a vehicle for continued abuse. He may question them about your activities, blame you for breaking up the family, and attempt to convince the children you don't love them.

If you believe the visitation rights granted the father place the children or you in further danger, your best course of action is to continue to fight the decision in court. This can be extremely expensive, but many organizations and legal clinics provide this form of assistance for little or no fee (see chapter 12, "Practical Considerations").

Talking to the Children

In deciding how to explain to the children the pain, abuse, and emotional trauma they have seen, you should rely on your own judgment and intuition relative to their ages to decide what they need and want to hear. However, some basic principles can be incorporated into all discussions.

1. Your children have a right to and a need for truthful, age-appropriate information about what they witnessed and why the abuser is not living with them anymore. Younger children will usually accept an explanation about how mad Daddy got sometimes and how both parents decided it was better if they lived apart. Older children can usually understand and handle the concept that their father had tendencies to be jealous, controlling, or violent and, therefore, it was necessary

for him to live away from the family. As was discussed in the previous two sections, children need to be told, as accurately as possible, what threat, if any, your abuser poses to them now.

2. Your children, especially the younger ones, still love their daddy, although they have seen him do terrible things to you and, perhaps, to them. They need to be allowed to have these feelings.

3. Telling the children that their father is a "bad" person will probably only further upset and confuse the children and will not be helpful in the long run. It's better to talk to them about his *behaviors* (yelling, threatening, hitting) and how they were difficult, dangerous, or scary, rather than making sweeping statements about his character.

4. Children need to be told firmly and frequently they are safe (refer to chapter 2, "Are You Out of Danger Now?") and you will always be there for them. Obviously, there are no absolute guarantees in life, but this is a fundamental message all children need in their lives, regardless of the abuse.

5. Children need to feel they are loved unconditionally by you. You can help them to feel this by telling them often and directly. Try to take the time to look into the child's eyes, touch or hold the child, and say, "I love you." This goes much farther than a quick perfunctory "Love you . . ." as you say goodnight and turn off the light. Also, when disciplining them, be sure to let them know that you are displeased with their behavior, not with them as people. Say, "I'm very upset that you did that," not "You are so stupid to have done that."

6. Children need to be reassured in every possible way that the abuse and the breakup of the relationship were not their fault. Try not to wait for them to bring this up, but instead talk to each child individually to explain that the problem was with your abuser and between him and you. Tell each child in a way he or she can understand that the children did

nothing wrong and that they are not to blame for their father's leaving.

7. Children (especially boys) should be shown that abuse and violence in all forms is wrong. This is a difficult order in a culture that glorifies violence and is built on a violent past (see chapter 3, "How Could This Have Happened?"). Try to find the time to watch TV and videos with your kids. Discuss violence that is portrayed in the media. When they are old enough to understand, talk to them about how that violence is related to the violence they have experienced personally in their lives. Let them know that they can play an effective role in reducing and preventing violence not just in their own lives but in the society in general.

8. Children (especially girls) should learn from their mother that they must never accept such abusive behavior and that they have a right to be loved and not harmed. It's probably better not to try to hide or deny what happened to you and them but instead to discuss it as openly as is appropriate and use it as an example of totally unacceptable behavior in any relationship.

9. Children need to be told, in all possible ways, that the abuse they saw or experienced in your relationship is wrong, it should never happen to anyone, and it has no place in a loving relationship.

Should You Seek Professional Help for Your Children?

If you have a child who appears to be especially affected by the abuse, specially trained therapists can help the child deal with the trauma of domestic violence. Some general guidelines can assist you in estimating your children's need for outside help (these guidelines appear in greater detail in the exercise at the end of this chapter). Consider the various emotional, psychological, and behavioral symptoms discussed earlier. Note any of the symptoms you see in your child. Then consider each of the observed signs on three dimensions.

The first dimension is *frequency*. How often does your child display a particular symptom? Generally, the more often a symptom appears, the greater the need for some kind of treatment. Next is *intensity*. How strong is the symptom when it appears? If the emotion, the psychological difficulty, or the behavior is especially intense, that is, clearly identifiable and impossible to ignore, a greater need for professional intervention may be indicated.

Finally, is the dimension of *interference with functioning*. To what extent are the symptoms interfering with your child's daily life in school, at home, with friends, and his or her relationship with you? If several symptoms rate high on these dimensions, an appointment with a professional counselor might be a very good idea.

How to Find Help for Your Children

There are several ways to locate counselors who are specifically trained to deal with postabuse problems. The listings in the yellow pages in most cities and towns include sections for counselors and therapists. These will usually be found under "Marriage, Family, and Child Counselors," "Mental Health Services," "Psychologists," "Psychotherapy," "Social Workers," "Social Service Agencies," or "Clinics." Look for specific information in the listings that indicates a specialty in family violence or abuse issues. If you are not sure which therapists in your area have this specialized training, check with your local domestic violence crisis center or abuse hotline for specific recommendations and referrals. Many counselors provide services on a sliding scale, meaning that the fees they charge will be reduced for those clients with lower incomes.

If you continue to have difficulty finding a qualified professional to assist your children, call the National Domestic Violence Hotline at 1-800-799-SAFE. In addition to crisis intervention information, the hotline also maintains an extensive list of counseling resources by city and state and should be able to provide referrals in your area.

If you think one or more of your children may need some professional assistance, but you are not sure, one way to find out is to schedule a preliminary visit with a family violence or abuse counselor for evaluation and assessment. If the therapist concludes that the child is doing well and does not need further intervention, you will feel a weight has been lifted from your shoulders. On the other hand, if the outcome of the assessment suggests counseling is needed, you will then be clear about needing to provide it (refer to chapter 13, "Beginning to Heal," for additional information on obtaining counseling).

Your children are going through this healing process with you. As you feel stronger and more able to cope with life, you model these successes for your children. You will help them to recover, and they, in turn, will help you.

Child Assessment

Below is a list of emotional, psychological, and behavioral difficulties children sometimes experience in the aftermath of an abusive relationship. Using your own best judgment, rate each item on the list in *all three dimensions* using *all* of the following scales for each of your children:

NEARLY NEVER   *VERY OFTEN*

| 1 | 2 | 3 | 4 | 5 | 6 | 7 | 8 | 9 | 10 |

FREQUENCY OF SYMPTOM

EXTREMELY MILD   *EXTREMELY INTENSE*

| 1 | 2 | 3 | 4 | 5 | 6 | 7 | 8 | 9 | 10 |

INTENSITY OF SYMPTOM

ALMOST NONE   *NEARLY CONSTANT*

| 1 | 2 | 3 | 4 | 5 | 6 | 7 | 8 | 9 | 10 |

INTERFERENCE WITH DESIRED FUNCTIONING

Symptom	*Frequency* *1–10*	*Intensity* *1–10*	*Interference* *1–10*
Suicidal thoughts**	_____	_____	_____
Alcohol abuse**	_____	_____	_____
Other drug abuse**	_____	_____	_____
Animal cruelty**	_____	_____	_____
Self-injury**	_____	_____	_____
Anxiety	_____	_____	_____
Social withdrawal	_____	_____	_____
Crying	_____	_____	_____
Not having fun	_____	_____	_____
Sleep problems	_____	_____	_____
Eating problems	_____	_____	_____
Stuttering	_____	_____	_____
Self-blame	_____	_____	_____
Guilt	_____	_____	_____

Fear of abandonment	_____	_____	_____
Low self-esteem	_____	_____	_____
Delays in motor skills	_____	_____	_____
Verbal language delays	_____	_____	_____
Psychosomatic illness	_____	_____	_____
Poor impulse control	_____	_____	_____
Tantrums	_____	_____	_____
Fighting with siblings	_____	_____	_____
Destroying property	_____	_____	_____
Throwing objects	_____	_____	_____

Note 1: The first five items marked with a (**) are of especially great concern. If your child is experiencing any of these, *regardless of the degree*, you need to consider immediate professional support.

Note 2: If your child scores low on this scale, but you feel he or she needs some professional assistance, follow your instincts. No single scale can measure such a need with 100 percent accuracy and no one knows your child better than you.

When you have finished, analyze your ratings for all the symptoms on all three dimensions. Use the following guidelines for interpreting your ratings and making decisions about your child's need for counseling.

♦ Ratings below 3 on any single item in any of the columns indicate that there may be little need for concern (except for the items marked with **).

♦ A rating of 3 to 4 on any single item in any column indicates a need to be mildly concerned about these behaviors. Counseling may not be needed at this time, but it would be a good idea to be alert to these behaviors in the future.

♦ A rating of 5 to 6 on any single item in any column indicates a need for moderate concern about these behaviors. Counseling might be helpful now in dealing with them and preventing them from becoming worse.

♦ Scores of 7 or higher on any single item in any column indicate a serious problem may exist. Your child would benefit greatly by receiving counseling now or in the very near future.

11

The Reactions of Others

Everyone couldn't stop putting him down. I've been out of the relationship for six months now. I really don't want to keep hearing about how awful he was.

BETHANY, AGE 32

Whenever I talk about what happened, I can see it in their eyes. They may not say it, but I can see they're thinking I was crazy to have stayed with him for so long.

MELA, AGE 53

With some of my friends, it's as though he didn't do anything wrong. They talk about how "happy" we were at first and about how funny or attractive he is. How can they ignore what he did to me?

LINDSEY, AGE 23

Myth: Everyone who is your true friend will understand and accept what happened in your relationship without question.

Myth: It's better to have family around you even if they hurt you.

Myth: All your friends and family will deal with the aftermath of the abuse the same as you.

*A*s you rebuild your new life, you will need to decide who will be part of it and who won't. These decisions are completely up to you, and they can be among the most difficult you will make. Making judgments about keeping people in your life will take time and careful introspection. The only sure thing is that you need others in your life to support you, to be friends with you, and to love you.

Three crucial questions you should ask when trying to decide if you want someone to be a part of your life now and in the future are:

1. Is this person someone who can support and love you?
2. Does this person create positive feelings about who you are and the choices you have made in freeing yourself from an abusive relationship?
3. Can you trust this person completely?

If you can answer these questions, your decision should be easier. However, the answers may not always come easily.

People Who Failed to Support You in the Past

All of us experience difficult times in our lives. And most of us believe our family and friends will always be there for us. We expect they will love and support us no matter what. When they let us down, we can feel devastated. The anger, disappointment, and loss we experience in those situations can make any future intimate bond with them almost impossible.

People who were not there for you during your abusive relationship are often the most difficult to keep in your life. They may include your family members, his family members, friends, or coworkers. A variety of reasons exist for why they let you down, but the fact remains, they were not there when you needed them.

You may discover you want nothing to do with those who abandoned you during the abusive relationship. If you believe you cannot move past your negative feelings toward them, cutting all ties may be your only available course of action. In some cases, however, you may decide you need time to heal from your wounds and reevaluate your relationship with them.

If you decide you want some of these people to remain in your life, it will be important to find ways to communicate to them your feelings about what happened. If you continue to harbor adverse feelings toward them and do not openly deal with it, those feelings are sure to surface in unproductive ways. Try talking to them about your feelings and about their lack of support. See if you can come to an understanding that truly allows your differences to be in the past. If you can accomplish this, you will have created a strong friendship and support that may last for the rest of your life.

Those Who Overlooked the Abuse

It may help to understand why some people failed to support you. One reason may be that they didn't believe the abuse was happening or minimized how bad it was. If this rings true, think about why they doubted you. If they are his relatives, they were probably able only to see him as a perfect son, brother, or grandson. He probably hid his controlling and abusive side from them so well and for so long they were convinced that "he could never do a thing like that." If he is like most abusers, he was a master at concealing his abusive side.

Some people may defend him with their belief that he had a hard life growing up and really, deep down, he loves you. They may have gone to great lengths to explain to you all of the difficulties your abuser experienced in his life and how he worked so hard to overcome them. They probably told you how good you were for him and how much he needed you. They had a way of making you feel guilty for condemning him for the abuse.

These people are unlikely to see your experience any differently now. In fact, he has probably convinced them you were at fault for the failure of the relationship. Unless something very convincing has altered their beliefs, their judgments of you and the relationship may never change. You need to decide if keeping such people in your life has sufficient value.

Those Who Blamed You

Some people not only didn't support you but actually blamed you! These people, when you told them about an incident of abuse, immediately asked something like, "What did you do to make him so mad?" They gave you advice about how relationships are difficult and how you needed to stick it out and try harder. Some of them even told you the abuse was his right and you are the one who must change your attitudes and behaviors to remedy the problem.

It's important for you to look at the reasons these people behaved this way. Try not to obsess about the past, but try to determine how they are likely to act in the future. You may need to decide if you can forgive them (and this may not be possible for you), and assess whether or not a future relationship with them is in your best interests (see Do I Need to Forgive? later in this chapter).

Those who have an ingrained belief that men can do whatever they want in a relationship are probably not people you want in your life. They will remind you forever that you made a mistake, in their eyes, when you left your abuser. Also, they may judge your future relationships and interfere with your need to make the choices that are best for you.

You may feel uncomfortable breaking off unwanted relationships because they are family members or because you fear hurting their feelings. But no one should ever feel obligated to be close with those who do not enhance their life. If your instincts tell you they are not worth your time and trouble, follow those instincts.

Look at it this way: You endured so much pain, and it took such strength and courage to get out of that abusive relationship, all of your new relationships should be on your terms. This is not selfish or egotistical. It is taking care of you. You need to recognize the qualities you need from your close relationships and ensure they are present in relationships you decide to maintain. You will also need to set boundaries for what you will not accept.

Those Who Did Not Know How to Help

Many of your friends and family members may fall into this category. They really love you and wanted to help you in your time of need. Nevertheless, they simply did not know what to say or do. Their intentions were good, but they were unable to improve your situation.

A common example of this involves family and friends who were always urging you to leave him. They could not understand why that was so difficult and complex an issue for you. Perhaps, as time went on and you were still in the relationship, they began to be less sympathetic about the abuse. Even if they didn't say so directly, it seemed to you that they were thinking, "I told you so." Eventually, their opinions made you feel increasingly at fault and less and less comfortable confiding in them.

Now that you have left that relationship, reestablishing relationships with these friends may be difficult. They may go to great lengths to remind you how awful your relationship was and throw in comments such as "I'll never understand why you stayed with him for so long" or "I would never have put up with that." You may see these people as your friends, but you find yourself frequently defensive and uncomfortable around them. Explaining to them over and over that getting out wasn't all that easy and was much more complicated than they could ever imagine is wearing you out.

If you are trying to decide whether to keep these people in your life, you have to examine the emotional impact they have on you now. Some of these friends may give you support, respect, and friendship despite their past shortcomings. With some of them, you may be able to tune out their shortsightedness and cherish the good parts of your relationship.

On the other hand, if you find their judgmental view of the abusive relationship negates the positives, you may have to reexamine the value of their friendship to you. You can try talking with these friends and explaining to them how their attitudes affect you; tell them that when they judge your actions you feel guilty, sad, and angry. If they seem to get it, you can try making them allies in your healing process. Explain that you realize abusive relationships can be difficult to understand, but now that you are out, you need to move on and avoid dwelling on the past. Although they weren't there for you in the past, they may be able to be here for you now.

Those Who Knew but Did Nothing

What about the people who knew about the abuse but chose to ignore it? The knowledge of what he was doing may have been too painful for them to accept. They may have felt they didn't know what to say or do and, therefore, did nothing. Unfortunately, many friends and family members of abused women, when questioned later, say they didn't want to intrude or didn't want to lose the friendship by interfering.

Perhaps their silent acceptance of the abuse now feels like a betrayal. It's easy, once you are out, to think that if only someone had been there for you, it would have been different. But is that really true? Assessing your relationships with these "silent" friends involves evaluating whether their intervention in the abuse would have changed anything. Could they have said or done anything to stop the abuse? See if you can talk with these friends about their silence. Don't confront or accuse them, but just ask them why they didn't talk about it with you. You may be surprised by their answer.

Some might insist they did acknowledge the abuse to you. They might very well assert they remember being empathetic often, but they always got the feeling *you* didn't want to discuss it. Abuse is a very difficult subject to bring up with someone you love. You may fear alienating or angering that person. Some of your friends may have feared losing you if they were to push the subject. They may say they were there for you but left it up to you to initiate discussion about the abuse. They may have seen your relationship as personal and they had no business intruding.

If you decide to mend these relationships, being honest will be important. You can talk about how you appreciate their willingness to talk now and focus on whatever support they gave you. You may want to tell them you understand how terribly difficult it was for them to say anything. Listening, without becoming defensive, to their version of past events can be helpful. They may have given you subtle signs of concern, but you were in no condition at the time to pick up on them. If you can relieve the tension and open up to each other, these may be among your best future friends.

Those Who Told You What to Do

It's possible you had some friends and family members who believed they were going to be the ones to rescue you. They probably felt they were your only real supporters because they told you exactly what you should and should not do to fix the problem. They were free with their advice and always seemed to know what was best for you.

These people probably had your welfare at heart. They believed if you "didn't know what was good for you," they would help you understand. They felt they knew what was wrong or right and they would guide you in the best direction. Unfortunately, without realizing it, they may have become just what you did not need: people trying to control your life.

Now that you are out of the abusive relationship and in charge of your life, your contacts with this group of people may feel strained. They may still want to control you. It probably feels controlling if they are telling you what you should be doing or feeling, such as "You're not going to allow the children to see him, are you?" or "It's too soon for you to date again. What will people think?" These judgmental comments may undermine your confidence to make decisions that are best for you and take charge of your life.

Everyone at times may get a bit too "pushy" with a friend they believe is in trouble or in pain. All of us may try to guide that person to a better situation. It often makes sense for people who are having a difficult time to take the insights and opinions of those they trust into consideration. These people, however, after offering their wisdom and advice, should then be able and willing to step back and allow you to guide your own life. If they can do that, they may become a positive part of your support system. If they can't, it may be a warning sign of too much external control.

Do I Need to Forgive?

You do not *owe* anyone your forgiveness. Forgiveness is not necessary for everyone in order to heal. You alone can decide whom to forgive.

Did you grow up hearing it is always better to forgive and forget? Were you raised to believe that happiness requires acceptance of others' faults? Have you always believed it's necessary to forgive so that you can "move on"?

Forgiveness is a very complicated issue. Despite what some may say, forgiving everyone for their past actions is not always a requirement for healing. The decision to forgive rests on three conditions:

1. whether or not you believe what they did (or didn't do) were forgivable acts,

2. whether or not you feel it will help in your healing to forgive them, and

3. whether or not you feel ready to forgive. A "right" time for forgiveness or any absolute rule about whom you must forgive does not exist.

Some people forgive easily. Others hold on to frustrations and anger for a long time. Much of this may be attributed to differences in upbringing and experiences with forgiveness. Forgiving those who let you down may require time to heal those wounds. You need to move beyond the fear, anger, distrust, and sadness before you can think about forgiving. When you truly forgive someone, it must come from your heart and you must want to forgive.

Those Who Understood and Supported You

Having difficulties with those who really were there for you during the abuse doesn't seem to make much sense. These are the people who understood what you were going through and stayed with you throughout. They didn't seek to control your decision making or judge you. They simply let you know they cared and would always be there for you no matter what. These individuals are likely to continue to be your closest friends and relatives now. However, the transition to a postrelationship friend is not always as smooth as you might expect.

Maybe you "disappeared" during your relationship and lost contact with them because your abuser would not allow you to have friends of your own. This is very common in unhealthy, controlling relationships. Maybe you didn't want to burden them with your problems and couldn't bear for them to know how much he was hurting you. Or maybe you were afraid they would try to come to your rescue and make things worse by forcing you to take steps that you were not ready to take. As you look back on this now, you may feel guilty about excluding them for so long.

Maybe you didn't actually disappear, but instead you were only partially and selectively truthful with them. You probably remember times when they asked you about why you refused to go somewhere with them, why you had to call home so often when you were out, or how you got that bruise on your arm. Now you may feel that you were not a good friend to them because you lied to them so often.

Perhaps you didn't hide anything from those friends. They were the ones you ran to when things got too bad. They comforted you, listened to you, and empathized with you, over and over again. Then, each time, you'd go back to your abuser. You could see the disbelief, sadness, and maybe disapproval in their eyes when you talked to him on the phone and agreed to go back. They may have told you how afraid they were for you and how much they worried about you. Looking back, you are amazed that anyone could have "put up" with you for so long. When you look at it now, it seems like a miracle that they remained so loyal and understanding.

Now that you are finally out of that abusive relationship, you might find yourself feeling guilty and embarrassed around these friends. You need to remind yourself, although you wish you had not put them through all of that, you had no other choice at the time. If you had confided in them completely, hiding your confessions from your abuser might have been too difficult for you. If he found out, the abuse would have become much worse and you might not have been able to talk to them at all.

Perhaps you also needed to convince yourself it wasn't really all that bad, so you softened your experience when you talked to them. Whatever the reason, you need to move beyond the guilt. You deserve all the benefits of their friendship and your friends deserve to have yours. In those close, intimate friendships, guilt and embarrassment should not play a major role. You did the best you could and they know that.

It is never too late to thank these people for all they did for you. Let them know how much they meant and mean to you. You don't need to give them expensive gifts or find the perfect words. Just say what is in your heart. If saying these things directly to them is difficult for you, send them a card, a note, or even an e-mail expressing your gratitude. Let them know that even the little things—the small gestures, their words of encouragement—were of enormous help to you in your time of need.

Finding New Friends and Supports

Now that you are out of your abusive relationship, the characteristics you seek in new friendships might be a bit different. You might be a little (or a lot) less trusting, and, therefore, you now take more time to decide how close to let people get to you. Nothing is wrong with being cautious in new relationships. Also, nothing is wrong with making conscious choices about whom you allow into your life.

Your needs right now may be different from those of others around you. New people in your life may not know exactly what it is you need or want from them. It will be up to you to educate them about how they can best be your friends. This may mean telling them if, when, and how to ask about your past, how to talk to you about your current life, and about what you really need in a friendship (trust, consistency, honesty, etc.).

If you are still experiencing profound emotions related to the abuse, letting others in who don't understand may be difficult (see chapter 7, "When Feelings Overwhelm You"). Again, it's smart to be cautious in new relationships, but, at the same time, building new support networks is important. Good people exist who can truly be there for you. You need to make sure you don't build walls preventing anyone new from coming in. If you put up barriers, in the end you, and they, lose.

Evaluating Your Relationships

As you have seen throughout this book, evaluating issues in your life is sometimes easier if you commit them to paper. This is true even when reviewing your relationships with others. No absolute method for rating your relationships exists. (Gee, Joey must be a better friend than Heather. She rated a 92, and Heather was only a 78!) However, a general analysis to determine if you are receiving what you need from them is possible. The following exercise will help you to do this. For each relationship you are questioning, complete the following form.

Person's name or initials _____

Characteristic or feature	*All the time*	*Some of the time*	*Never*
Supportive of me in the past	_____	_____	_____
Supportive of me now	_____	_____	_____
Made a real effort to be there for me during the abuse	_____	_____	_____
Is honest	_____	_____	_____
Is reliable	_____	_____	_____
Is trustworthy	_____	_____	_____
Values me as a person	_____	_____	_____
Recognizes the seriousness of what I've been through	_____	_____	_____
Empathizes with my current emotions	_____	_____	_____
Wants to help but not control me	_____	_____	_____

Characteristic or feature	All the time	Some of the time	Never
Does not judge me	_____	_____	_____
Has my best interests at heart	_____	_____	_____
Other	_____	_____	_____

Now review your answers. How does this friend or family member measure up? Do your ratings agree with your intuitive feelings about this person? Use this form to begin to evaluate each of the relationships you are questioning. You can also use it to help obtain an objective view of new acquaintances who may be possible future friends.

Looking Forward

12

Practical Considerations

After I left, I felt like a lost soul; I didn't have a job, I didn't have any credit, I didn't know how I was going to survive.

JESSICA, AGE 29

He controlled everything, the checkbook, the bills, the bank accounts. When I left, I was starting over with zero, which felt awful at my age.

ANNE, AGE 40

After getting out, I needed a lot of help. I was afraid for our safety and I was really worried that I might lose my kids.

BLANCA, AGE 31

Myth: Once you are free from the abuse, the rest of life will take care of itself.

Myth: It's such a relief to be away from your abuser that the details of daily life seem easy.

Myth: Survivors of domestic violence are victims who just can't make it on their own.

One of the reasons some women return to their abusers is that the everyday demands of life on their own feel overwhelming. If you are like most survivors of abuse, you know your former partner not only sought to control you but also made sure he was in charge of nearly all aspects of the relationship. He probably carefully managed access to all the family money. Bank and credit card accounts may all have been in his name. He wanted you to be as dependent upon him as possible and may have used financial tactics to help ensure your dependence. On the other hand, some abusers do not contribute financially and require their partners to provide necessary income. If this was true in your relationship, he may still have exerted control over all the money you earned and how it was spent.

Many women in abusive relationships find themselves cut off from the outside world. Your abuser's demands may have limited you to specific activities and deviating from those allowed behaviors was not worth the risk of triggering an abusive episode. Your shrinking self-esteem and self-confidence may have made you feel insecure and timid when you were out in the community.

The effects of losing your financial independence and familiar daily activities emerge when you have finally left your abuser. If you are experiencing thoughts such as "Oh, my God! How do I put my life in order all by myself?", you know the feeling. You are building a new life. This is an emotional healing process, but it also entails countless practical challenges. Unfortunately, it is the fear of facing these practicalities that drives some survivors back to their former partners and continued, escalating abuse.

This chapter is devoted to discussing some of these basic life issues and to offering you some guidelines and reassurance that you can handle them and become a self-sufficient person.

Legal Issues

Have you felt the need for legal assistance in the aftermath of your abusive relationship? If you have, you are not alone. Important legal matters are often part and parcel of the process of terminating relationships involving abuse. These include—but are not limited to—obtaining and enforcing a temporary restraining order, filing separation and divorce documents, dealing with child custody issues, tax assistance, establishing financial independence, and documenting the abuse for legal purposes. A discussion of these legal issues in more detail will be followed by detailed information on locating and affording legal assistance.

Temporary Restraining Orders

You may already be aware of the *temporary restraining order* (TRO), also called a stay-away order or protection order (this was discussed in chapter 2, "Are You Out of Danger Now?"). A temporary restraining order is issued by a judge often without a formal hearing and is intended to protect you and your children from the actions of your abuser. TROs are issued for a variety of purposes including those designed to: stop your former partner from abusing, threatening, or interfering with you and your children; forbid the abuser to enter your home, school, place of business, or other specified location; order the abuser out of your home; require police to stand guard while you remove personal belongings from the home; and give you temporary legal custody of your children.

A violation of the restraining order is a misdemeanor, and the police may arrest the abuser even if they did not witness the violation. Felony charges may also be brought. Fear of arrest may be enough reason for many abusers to obey the order, but a temporary restraining order is *no guarantee* of safety for the abuser's victims.

The exact characteristics of TROs, the details of obtaining them, and the specific penalties for violation vary somewhat from state to state. Therefore, a good lawyer can often be of great help in obtaining one quickly and smoothly and ensuring you know how to report any violations of the order. However, a lawyer is not necessary for you to seek a TRO. You can also usually receive assistance from your local police department or domestic violence shelters and organizations in your area.

Court Proceedings

Separation and divorce papers can be extremely complicated and complex, especially when they involve property disputes and child custody issues. This process can feel even more overwhelming if you are working on recovering emotionally from your relationship. Typically, abusers will resist divorce proceedings.

If your abuser is the legal father of the children and your abuse cannot be clearly proved, most courts will require some form of joint custody or visitation arrangement. This can be a frightening prospect when you know how abusive and dangerous your ex-partner can be. A lawyer can help ensure your rights are protected in divorce, custody, or visitation matters.

Financial-Legal Issues

You may need a lawyer to untangle you financially from your abuser and help you to establish your economic independence. This may be especially tricky if you had little control or knowledge of your finances during the relationship. However, even if you knew a great deal about how he was spending your money, creating debt, or establishing credit, the financial legacy of your relationship can be extremely complex and emotionally draining.

If you were married to your abuser, you may be liable for his debts. Even if you were not married, abusers sometimes coerce their partners to cosign for loans and credit purchases. Moreover, you may have felt helpless to refuse to sign fraudulent joint tax returns during the relationship, placing you at risk of IRS actions. Any credit that was established during your relationship may be in his name. Legal procedures exist for separating his credit history from yours and establishing your own credit standing.

Criminal Charges

Finally, relationship violence is a crime. In some cases, proving the violence occurred and demonstrating the severity of it is difficult. If prosecuting your abuser is an option, you may need a lawyer to help you make the strongest case possible for arrest, trial, conviction, and prison.

Obtaining Legal Help

You may be thinking you need legal help and advice, for some of the reasons discussed in the previous section, but you have no idea how to find it or you doubt you can afford it. So how do you go about obtaining a lawyer who is knowledgeable about domestic violence issues, skilled in court, and affordable? Fortunately, awareness of domestic violence issues within the legal community has created various avenues for obtaining competent legal advice and representation at low or no cost. You just need to know how find those avenues.

Centered in the Washington, DC, area, is a national organization called Legal Aid for Abused Women (LAAW). LAAW offers legal services for victims of abusive relationships and provides a revolving fund for legal aid. LAAW can be reached at 703-837-8993.

Another national organization dedicated to providing assistance to victims of abuse is the American Bar Association's Commission on Domestic Violence. On its very informative Web site (www.abanet.org/domviol/), it provides numbers for abuse hotlines and lawyer referrals for all types of legal problems by state. If you do not have access to a computer at home or work, most local libraries have free Internet access. If you are not familiar with the Internet, the library staff will show you how to use the computer to access the myriad of resources on the World Wide Web. The commission may also be reached by phone at 312-988-5760.

Many cities, counties, and law schools sponsor legal aid clinics. These clinics are often open a limited number of hours each week and are staffed by advanced law students or practicing or retired lawyers who are volunteering their time. These clinics can be found in the yellow pages under "Legal Aid" or by calling a local law school or women's shelter. If you contact a legal aid clinic, be sure to ask for a volunteer who is specifically trained to handle domestic violence cases.

Additionally, in many cities and towns there are *court advocates* who can help you with complicated legal issues. Court advocates are free and will not influence your decisions in any way. Their role is to assist you in working through emotionally draining legal processes. Contact your local court or sexual assault and domestic violence crisis center to find out if such free help exists in your area.

Finally, you can obtain more information on sources for legal assistance from the National Domestic Violence Hotline at 1-800-799-SAFE.

Financial Assistance: Friends and Family

If you are like many women who escape an abusive partner, you may have found yourself in a difficult financial situation. As was mentioned earlier, your abuser may have tightly controlled the money in your relationship as part of his overall control of you, and when you left, he made sure that you had no access to savings or checking accounts. Furthermore, you may not be employed or the income from your job may be insufficient to support you and your children. The fear of poverty should not force you to return to your abuser. Therefore, it is important for you to get back on your feet financially as soon as possible.

Do you have friends or family who may be willing to help you out? Maybe some have already offered. This is probably a good time to ask for help or take them up on their offers. Many people feel embarrassed to take money from others, but this is a time for you to focus on your emotional healing. Close friends and relatives are probably relieved you are out of that terrible situation and would really like to help you. If accepting a gift makes you too uncomfortable, agree to take the money as a loan and offer a written promise to repay it. Keep in mind that accepting help from others is not selfish or weak but a frank acknowledgment of your current, *temporary* crisis.

What if you, like most of us, don't have people lined up to give or lend you money? There are several other possible routes you can take to smooth out your financial crisis. One source of help is abused- or battered-women's shelters. These organizations often have a fund from which money can be loaned or given to help survivors through the immediate crisis. If the shelters in your area do not have such a fund, they will at least provide food and shelter until you can find a source of income.

Also, a lawyer can assist you in gaining access to any money that is rightfully yours but is being kept from you by your former abuser. Specific filings can be made to the court forcing your partner to release such funds to you.

Finding Employment

If you do not have a job already and if your situation allows, you may want to consider obtaining work as soon as you can. While this is often easier said than done, you might want to think about accepting a job that is not ideal for you or is perhaps more menial than you deserve, so that you can begin to receive a check and, one hopes, some benefits. It is also a boost to your self-esteem and self-confidence to be working and bringing home a paycheck. You do not have to think of this as a permanent position; it can be just a job to help you get by until you can find something better.

It is common for survivors of abusive relationships to have developed few job skills. This is another tactic abusers use to keep their partners wholly dependent on them. If you are in such a position, you might want to consider acquiring skills or obtaining some education toward a career that interests you. As long as you are earning enough to get by for now, you can take your time cultivating your new skills and talents. During this time of healing, there is no need to feel pressured to get a degree or to find your ideal career. It is becoming very common for adults of all ages to return to school through community college, 4-year college, and university programs. You can approach your education slowly, on a part-time basis or by taking just one course at a time. Education does not have to be expensive. Depending on your state, community college enrollment is very inexpensive or even free.

In addition to their many counseling, support, and prevention services, most abused- or battered-women's agencies and shelters offer job training programs, including skills assessment, strategies for obtaining and keeping jobs, résumé preparation, and job placement services with ties to potential employers in the community. They are there to help you, and sometimes the best course of action you can take is to let them.

Public Sources of Financial Assistance

Many governmental programs at the federal, state, and local levels are designed to help survivors of domestic abuse and violence in many ways. At the federal and state levels, these include public assistance benefits (welfare), food stamp programs, Medicaid benefits, Social Security Disability Insurance (SSD) Benefits, Supplemental Security Income (SSI) Benefits, and Temporary Assistance for Needy Families (TANF), the new federal welfare program for families with children. You may qualify for one or more of these programs.

Most state and local governments offer additional programs as well. It can be difficult to find these programs, to determine the one for which you may qualify, and to fill out and submit the appropriate forms needed to receive the assistance. Domestic violence shelters and organizations have individuals on their staffs who can advise and help you apply for these government assistance programs. In addition, there are specific government offices in your town or county seat that are in charge of administering these funds. While they may not always offer personalized service, they can provide you with the forms and instructions you will need to begin the application process.

Accessing public assistance programs is another way an attorney can be of great benefit to you. Attorneys who donate their time and energy to domestic violence victims are familiar with all these programs and the process of applying for them.

You may be hesitant to apply for public assistance because you perceive that social stigmas are attached to being a "welfare recipient." But if you stop to think about it, these programs have been developed to help those who are in situations such as yours. You are not taking undue advantage of them. You are using them as they were intended to be used: to support you and your children while you are in transition from your old, unhealthy life to your new, productive one.

Reestablishing Credit

If the credit cards, loans, mortgage, and so forth were in his name, you may be in the position of establishing your own credit starting from scratch. In today's economic environment, good credit is important for everything from obtaining a credit card to financing a car to buying a home someday. For most financial institutions, no credit history is the same as a bad one. Again, you can begin slowly to reestablish credit in your name. Lawyers and financial professionals who donate time and information to survivors of abuse are excellent resources for you in this regard. But you can take some steps on your own.

Many banks and credit unions will now offer *secured credit cards*. These are cards for which you deposit a specified amount, say, $200 or $300, into a savings account that serves as security for the credit card. The card's limit is the same as the amount you have placed on reserve. You use the card and make your monthly payments just as you would for any credit card. After a while, the bank sees that you are using the card responsibly and will convert the card to a standard credit account and your deposit is returned to you.

Other ways of establishing credit involve financing items from large retail stores. Often, large department chain stores will offer credit more readily to its customers than will banks and credit unions. If it is within your budget to finance a major purchase (such as a TV or stereo) and make all your payments on time, you will acquire a reference that will make future credit transactions easier.

Finally, car dealerships will usually extend financing to buyers who are without an extensive credit history. You may pay a higher interest rate than someone with a good credit history. However, if you can afford it, establishing your own credit standing may be worth a small extra monthly payment.

Health Care

Access to medical care including counseling during this period of healing from your abusive relationship is very important As discussed elsewhere in this book, many sources of stress exist in your life right now and you should not have to add doubts about medical care to the list. Health care is especially important at this time in your life because the stress of rebuilding your life often takes its toll on you physically and you may need attention for injuries sustained at the hands of your abuser. However, many survivors lose health care benefits when they leave the relationship because they were provided through his employer.

If you and your abuser are legally married, many states require that he continue to maintain health insurance benefits for you until such time as a final divorce settlement is completed. But because he may refuse this support, you may need to call on an attorney to assert your legal rights to medical insurance. Keep in mind, however, that he may be able to determine your whereabouts through his insurance statements.

Most battered-women's shelters have programs for providing at least basic medical care for their clients. This is often organized in much the same way as legal assistance, with physicians, nurse practitioners, and physician's assistants volunteering their time to treat medical problems and perform routine and preventive medical exams and services.

Additionally, federal and state programs such as those discussed in the previous section, including Medicaid and SSD, will often provide coverage for medical care to those who qualify. Finally, if you have a medical emergency and have no insurance or ability to pay out of pocket, go to the emergency department at your local hospital. Most hospitals will not refuse to treat emergencies regardless of the patient's insurance or financial status.

Accepting Help

As was mentioned before in this chapter, this early time of transition in your life may call for setting personal pride aside in deciding how to obtain the temporary help you need to survive. Perceiving the offers of assistance discussed here as "handouts" or as "charity" and feeling too proud, embarrassed, or ashamed to accept them is understandable and very common. However, allowing those who can help to do so may be part of your individual process of healing. You know reclaiming your life is not easy, and if individuals and organizations can make it a bit less difficult, take them up on their offers. Remember they *want* to help and your need for their help is only temporary. Maybe one day, when your life is back in order, you can repay them by working to help others who are going through what you are experiencing now.

How Much Money Do You *Need* to Survive?

This exercise may seem mundane compared with the other self-explorations in this book, but it is certainly no less important. If you can calculate approximately how much money you actually need on a monthly basis to survive at a basic level, it will be clearer to you what you must focus on for salary and financial assistance in various forms. So on the budget below estimate an amount for each item that applies to you (enter $0 for the items that do not apply or that you can do without). Be realistic! Don't underestimate, but focus on basic needs. This is a very detailed budget list so you can be as accurate as possible.

After you have estimated your monthly financial needs, there is another form to help you calculate your current and potential monthly income from various sources. These two basic pieces of information are necessary for you to make a plan that will lead to independence and self-sufficiency.

Budget item	*Estimated monthly amount*
GROCERY STORE	
Groceries	$_____.00
Toiletries	$_____.00
Other _____	$_____.00
MEDICAL	
Hospital	$_____.00
Physician	$_____.00
Dentist	$_____.00
Prescriptions/vitamins	$_____.00
Health insurance	$_____.00
Other _____	$_____.00
TRANSPORTATION	
Public transportation	$_____.00
Car payments	$_____.00
Taxes and fees	$_____.00
Tolls	$_____.00

Gas	$____.00
Auto maintenance	$____.00
Auto insurance	$____.00
Parking	$____.00
Parking permits	$____.00
Other _____	$____.00

CLOTHING

Mending/repair	$____.00
Dry cleaning/laundry	$____.00
New purchases/personal	$____.00
New purchases/work	$____.00
Other _____	$____.00

EDUCATION (YOU OR CHILD)

Education/training expenses	$____.00
Registration fees	$____.00
Tuition	$____.00
Books	$____.00
Room and board	$____.00
Miscellaneous	$____.00
Other _____	$____.00

CHILD EXPENSES

Day care	$____.00
Baby-sitting	$____.00
Clothing	$____.00
Diapers	$____.00
Formula	$____.00
Medicines	$____.00
Special food items (baby food)	$____.00
Other _____	$____.00

WORK-RELATED

Meals	$____.00
Office supplies	$____.00
Uniforms	$____.00
Union dues	$____.00
Other _____	$____.00

HOME EXPENSES

    Mortgage or rent $_____.00

    Gas $_____.00

    Electric $_____.00

    Heat $_____.00

    Water $_____.00

    Sewer $_____.00

    Insurance $_____.00

    Maintenance $_____.00

    Property tax $_____.00

    Snow plowing $_____.00

    Average phone use $_____.00

    Other _____ $_____.00

FIXED MONTHLY BILLS

    Credit card payments $_____.00

    Loan payments $_____.00

    Other _____ $_____.00

PETS

    Vet bills $_____.00

    Food $_____.00

    Board and care

    Other _____ $_____.00

MONTHLY POCKET MONEY ALLOWANCE $_____.00

TOTAL ESTIMATED MINIMUM
    MONTHLY EXPENSES $_____.00

CURRENT AND POTENTIAL SOURCES OF MONTHLY INCOME

Source	Current amount	Potential amount
Jobs	$_____.00	$_____.00
From savings	$_____.00	$_____.00
Interest	$_____.00	$_____.00
Child support	$_____.00	$_____.00
Alimony	$_____.00	$_____.00
From family	$_____.00	$_____.00
From friends	$_____.00	$_____.00
Public assistance (SSI, TANF, etc.)	$_____.00	$_____.00
Other	$_____.00	$_____.00

OTHER SOURCES OF INCOME (LIST):

_____	$_____.00	$_____.00
_____	$_____.00	$_____.00
_____	$_____.00	$_____.00
TOTALS	$_____.00	$_____.00

13

Beginning to Heal

I didn't realize I was depressed. One day my supervisor called me into her office and told me if my work didn't improve she would have to let me go. That was when I realized I needed help.

JEAN, AGE 48

I thought I had my anger under control. But when I realized I had spent twenty minutes yelling at my kids just because they were a little too noisy, I knew my anger was totally out of control.

KRISTIE, AGE 23

I'd wake up three or four times nearly every night in a cold sweat; my heart was pounding. I was a mess.

JACKIE, AGE 38

Myth: If you can't handle your problems by yourself, something must be seriously wrong with you.

Myth: If you need professional therapy, you must be crazy.

Myth: If you are strong enough, you can overcome anything on your own.

You may be wondering when you will finally respond with an *honest* "Fine!" when someone asks, "How are you?" As you are beginning to build your new life, you may be feeling a need to confront some of the troubling emotions that are plaguing you.

Three of the most overwhelming emotions are anger, depression, and anxiety. If these emotions become too severe, they can consume your life and derail your plans.

Anger

Nothing is intrinsically wrong with anger. Anger is a normal, healthy emotion. You have every right to feel anger toward your abuser. But if you feel the anger might be getting the better of you, it may be time to evaluate your anger and take some steps to gain some control over it.

How often are you angry? Is it interfering with your relationships with others? Is your anger always just below the surface, threatening to trigger negative thoughts and feelings? Do you find you obsess about how you might be able to get back at your abuser? If so, your anger may be to the point that it could destroy you if you don't learn to manage it.

If you feel you are angry all the time or if you are having any thoughts of *actually* injuring, maiming, or killing your abuser, you need to seek help immediately. Attacking your former abuser will only make your life worse and hurt others who love you. It's important to remind yourself that he just isn't worth it.

Most people learn as children that yelling, hitting, destroying property, and other violent acts are wrong. But at times, these behaviors, if performed in therapeutic, directed, and harmless ways, can help vent some of your stored-up anger.

If you ever feel you are so angry you want to scream, perhaps that's just what you should do. Find a place where no one will hear, and yell and scream as long as you want. Say whatever you are feeling. Don't hold back. Say everything you were never able to say to your abuser. Express how angry you are about what he did to you, about all he took from you. Consider inviting a trusted, understanding friend to join you so if you feel exhausted or tearful after this release, your friend can help you safely home.

If you don't have access to a place to yell, try screaming into a pillow. You might feel silly at first, but if you let yourself go, it will work wonders in ridding yourself of the accumulated rage. Yelling isn't a cure-all, but it can provide a safe emotional release.

Do you have times when you feel so angry you just want to hit someone? Hitting anyone, especially your former abuser, will only make the situation worse for you and could be dangerous. If you feel the need to hit, it's important to find ways of expressing this desire without causing yourself more harm. Hitting your bed, punching pillows can help release some of your fury. Hit something soft that will not hurt your hands. Striking a wall or door will only injure you, and you have been hurt enough. You may want to consider investing in a punching bag, which can be purchased in a variety of sizes and prices.

Are you able to express your angry thoughts or do you repress them? Every time you feel the anger surfacing, do you push it down and force yourself to think about something else? If you haven't been able to let the angry thoughts out, try writing them down. Write down everything that is causing your anger. If anger is an uncomfortable emotion for you, this may be difficult at first. Take it slowly if it helps. Start by writing down the one or two angry thoughts that come up most frequently. At first, these may be general causes such as "I'm angry about the abuse." As you continue to work on your list, you can refine them and make them much more specific. For example, specific anger-producing thoughts might include "I'm furious you imprisoned me by following me everywhere I went!" or "I hate you for breaking my favorite vase!"

Eventually, try to write everything that makes you angry. When you feel you are finished with your list for now, consider what you want to do with it. If you feel this has relieved much of your anger, you may want to put your list away for future reference. However, if you would rather get rid of this list, you might consider some therapeutic methods of disposing of it.

Take some time deciding what method of destroying your anger list will feel most cleansing. You can get rid of it all at once or in pieces. If you want to get rid of it all at once, try creating an anger-purging ceremony. You may want to make a statement or recite a poem you wrote expressing your feelings. On the other hand, you may want your feelings to pour out spontaneously. Your ceremony may involve tearing the list into as many small pieces as possible. You may then want to burn or bury it. Whatever you decide to do, the idea of this ritual is to help you release your anger and liberate yourself from all that rage.

If you think it would be more helpful for you to let go of the angry thoughts gradually, you may want to destroy parts of your list over time. One method of asserting your anger is to write one or more items from your anger list on pieces of tape. Stick the tape to the bottom of your shoes. Throughout the day, let your anger out by stomping your foot, walking especially hard, or stepping into something you would normally avoid. Or perhaps you want to tape items from your list onto each foot and do a "dance of healing." Be as creative as you want. Being physical with anger can bring welcome release.

Depression

Many common symptoms of depression were discussed in chapter 7, "When Feelings Overwhelm You." Changes in your eating and sleeping patterns, fatigue, feelings of hopelessness, and thoughts of hurting or killing yourself are all important signs of depression. Depressive symptoms may appear or intensify in the aftermath of an abusive relationship.

Mild Depression

How did you rate the various elements of depression in part III of the self-exploration at the end of chapter 7? If your ratings in that part of the exercise generally fell between 1 and 4, you may be somewhat depressed, but your mood probably isn't interfering seriously with your daily life or relationships with others. It probably feels manageable, although certainly not pleasurable. These are signs of mild depression. If your depression is mild, you can choose to take action to ease your sadness or you can wait for it to lift on its own. If you choose to deal actively with your depression, here are some effective ways to help soothe the pain.

One method of alleviating mild depression is to verbalize your sadness. Sometimes, merely expressing your emotions to someone who is supportive and will really listen can work wonders. Talking with a trusted friend or family member about your feelings can be very effective in easing the depression. If you are lacking the support you need at this time in your life, it's time to work on rebuilding those human resources of strength. Perhaps you can find support from family, friends, neighbors, or coworkers. But if not, consider joining a local club, organization, church group, or becoming involved in volunteer work. These activities, besides being fun and building your self-esteem, can assist you in meeting new people. Isolation and loneliness will usually intensify depression.

Another important part of coping with depression is accepting your feelings. Emotions are not right or wrong. If you are hiding from your emotions, not allowing yourself to feel, you could be making the depression worse. Hiding your true feelings will not make them go away.

Again, try writing all the reasons that you feel depressed. Acknowledge that what you have been through is more than sufficient reason to feel the way you do. Allow yourself to feel down, cry, and do whatever you need to do to be in touch with your emotions.

At the same time, make a point to do something pleasurable for yourself every day. Take a bubble bath, go for a long walk in the woods, talk with a friend on the phone, read a magazine, or work on an art or craft project. Be sure to allow yourself the pleasure of these activities on a regular basis. Your depression might blunt some of the pleasure in these activities for a while, but treat yourself to them anyway because they, in turn, will help defeat your depression.

Moderate or Severe Depression

If your scores in part III of the self-exploration exercise in chapter 7 generally fell above 4, this suggests that your depression may be moderate to severe. You may want to focus on more aggressive treatment. After an abusive relationship, depression is normal, but you shouldn't have to live with it forever. You can decide to get some help and start feeling better

How do you know when your depression is serious enough to require additional help? You are usually the best judge of that. Follow your instincts. Even if you're not sure whether or not you need counseling, consider seeing someone who can help you decide. Some general guidelines may help you determine just how serious your depression is and if you might need some professional help.

A key sign of more serious depression is that it is interfering noticeably with your daily activities. Are you finding it difficult to go to work or to perform up to your usual standards while on the job? Are routine, daily tasks such as making meals, taking care of your children, or maintaining your home beginning to feel overwhelming? Do you no longer find enjoyment in your favorite activities? These are indications the depression is worsening.

It's also important to pay attention to your sleeping and eating patterns. Sleeping too much, sleeping very little, or awakening very early in the morning without being able to go back to sleep are symptoms of serious depression. If you are eating very little or are eating much more than your usual amount, these may be signs that the depression is becoming more significant.

Suicidal Thoughts

Probably the most alarming sign of serious depression involves thoughts of hurting or killing yourself. Do you have days when you wish you would just not wake up the next morning? Do you sometimes hope an accident will relieve you of the burden of going on? At times, do you feel everyone would be better off if you were out of the picture? These thoughts should alert you to keep a very close eye on your depression. *If you begin to feel you might actually act on these thoughts, you need to get help immediately.* If you find yourself actually planning to kill yourself, thinking of methods you might use to kill yourself, or contemplating the right time to kill yourself, you should get help, now. Tell someone such as your doctor or a counselor, but don't wait until it's too late.

If you are experiencing symptoms of moderate or serious depression, it may not be the kind of problem you can defeat on your own. Seeking therapy does not mean that you are weak or crazy. You are having a normal reaction to a traumatic past. Obtaining counseling simply means you understand you are unable to work through all of your difficulties alone and are ready to allow a trained, caring professional guide you through them. Later in this chapter, we will discuss how you can find someone to help you.

Anxiety

If you feel your abuser continues to pose a real threat and you are concerned about protecting yourself and your children, then it is not just an anxiety problem. You are just being realistic and smart. But what if physical safety is not a concern? Does this mean that you don't have a right to be anxious? Of course not. Even if violence was never a part of your relationship, you may still feel anxious for many reasons now that you're out. If nothing else, starting your whole life over is enough to make anyone terribly anxious.

Everyone suffers from anxiety from time to time. When unexpected or uncontrollable events occur, we often feel anxious and worry about how everything will turn out. These normal feelings of anxiety are temporary and usually do not interfere with our lives in significant ways.

Some forms of anxiety, however, can be serious and debilitating. Often, you can identify a serious anxiety problem because the anxiety begins to take over. It is controlling you instead of you controlling it. This kind of anxiety often manifests itself in your interactions with others. Mild-to-moderate anxiety often causes you to be irritable and curt with those around you. You may appear more on edge and jumpy. Others may tell you to relax, "chill out," but you know that is easier said than done. You try to tell yourself to stop worrying so much, but if that works at all, it's a temporary fix.

Anxiety can also affect your mental processes. It can cause you to become stuck in a vicious cycle in which your attempt to stop your negative thoughts causes them to spin around and around in your mind even faster. You may find yourself thinking, "I can't do that," "Things will never work out," or "It's all just too much for me." These are signs your anxiety may be getting the better of you.

Anxiety also affects you physically. Do you have frequent stomachaches, neck or back pain, or headaches? Do you seem to get sick with colds and flu more than most people? Do you have frequent episodes of diarrhea or constipation? Does your heart race? Do you break out in cold sweats or hyperventilate? These can be signs of serious anxiety.

Severe anxiety can lead to very frightening episodes called *panic attacks*. Symptoms of panic attacks include shortness of breath, rapid heart rate, profuse sweating, tunnel vision, feelings of having a heart attack, a sense of "unreality," and a perception of impending death.

If these symptoms sound familiar, you may benefit from the stress-reducing techniques discussed in chapter 9, "Managing Your Stress." For any of the techniques discussed there to be effective, it's necessary to use them consistently and frequently. If you've tried those techniques, but your anxiety and panic persist or have intensified, it may be time to seek help. Nothing is wrong or crazy about suffering from anxiety. You are dealing with difficult, painful, and often frightening issues. Anxiety is one of many signs that you need to continue to heal from the abuse you suffered. Trained psychotherapists can help you learn to reduce and cope with your anxiety.

Getting Help

When we talk about getting help or seeking the assistance of a trained professional, we are referring to meeting with a counselor or therapist who specializes in working with women who have been in abusive relationships. Many people resist the idea of therapy, believing "only crazy people need that." Psychotherapy offers help for psychological or emotional problems, such as excessive anger, depression, or anxiety.

How can you tell if you should seek professional psychological help? For one thing, getting help does not mean you are crazy. On the contrary, most people seeking therapy are not mentally ill but are simply experiencing painful problems in their lives that they are unable to solve on their own. For most, however, deciding to get help for emotional pain is more difficult than seeking medical care.

When you are physically sick or injured, you usually experience relatively clear symptoms that serve as guidelines for calling the doctor. If you twist your knee skiing, the amount and duration of pain, swelling, discoloration, and loss of use will guide you in your decision whether or not to seek medical attention. Emotional problems may be just as painful, but most people are unclear what clues indicate a need for counseling.

How can you tell when the emotions you are feeling in the aftermath of an abusive relationship are serious enough to get help? As we've discussed throughout this chapter, if you analyze the intensity and duration of these emotions and the extent to which they are interfering with your present life and future goals, you should be able to tell if you would benefit from counseling.

Many sources for psychological support are available, some of which may be inexpensive or even free. You can obtain a referral from your local women's shelter, crisis center, or physician. You can also talk to people at your place of worship or ask friends and relatives who may have sought therapy themselves. If you are taking at least one class at a college or university, personal counseling services are often available there. It is important, however, that you find a counselor who is knowledgeable about controlling and abusive relationships.

Therapy works. Counselors, social workers, therapists, and psychologists are trained to help you deal with your anger, overcome your depression, and control your anxiety. Many people do not need to continue in therapy for years and years. In fact, progress can often be made in fewer than 10 sessions. Counseling is something you do for yourself. It is *completely* confidential. No one else ever needs to know. You may feel uncomfortable and a little frightened making that first appointment, but getting the help you need is an important step toward healing.

Do You Need Professional Help?(I)

This exercise is designed to help you decide if you want to consider counseling. Take your time as you go through this checklist. Be honest with yourself. You will only be hurting yourself by fudging the answers.

The more frequent the feelings and behaviors and the more checks you see when you are done, the greater the potential benefits from counseling. (**Note**: If you are having any suicidal thoughts, you should seek professional help immediately.) If you decide to seek therapy, you can complete this exercise anytime during your counseling process for a clear assessment of your progress.

As with many of the self-explorations in this book, we have included a second copy of this exercise so you can see how you are progressing. We recommend that you complete the checklist now and repeat it about 1 month from now. Our hope is that you will see improvement. If you do not see a decrease in the frequency of your painful emotions, that might be a useful signal to either seek or continue with professional counseling.

	Check the frequency of your behavior				
Behavior as of _____ *(date)*	*Very often*	*Often*	*Once in a while*	*Almost never*	*Never*
Angry verbal outbursts	_____	_____	_____	_____	_____
Feeling enraged	_____	_____	_____	_____	_____
Throwing things	_____	_____	_____	_____	_____
Hitting things	_____	_____	_____	_____	_____
Hitting people or animals**	_____	_____	_____	_____	_____
Feeling hopeless	_____	_____	_____	_____	_____
Feeling helpless	_____	_____	_____	_____	_____

Behavior as of _____(date)	Very often	Often	Once in a while	Almost never	Never
Changes in sleeping					
Changes in eating					
Feeling sad and "blue"					
Thoughts of self-injury					
Self-injurious actions**					
Suicide attempts**					
Suicidal thoughts**					
Excessive worrying					
Headaches					
Stomach problems					
Neck aches					
Backaches					
Anxiety					
Panic attacks					
Other					
Other					

Important note: If the items marked (**) are checked in any column except "Never," you should seek counseling immediately, regardless of your overall score on this exercise.

Interpreting Your Ratings:

No single test can absolutely determine your need for counseling. Your score on this self-exploration is just one factor in your decision to seek professional help at this complicated time in your life. Obviously the more frequently you suffer from any of the behaviors and feelings in the table, the more likely it is that some professional counseling will help you deal with them effectively.

Pay special attention to each item for which you checked

"Very often" or "Often." You are probably experiencing a great deal of pain from these feelings or behaviors. Most likely, your healing process will require some professional counseling sooner rather than later. These issues may be troubling you a great deal, and unless you can move toward resolving them, they could interfere with your successful healing process.

Also, notice the overall *number* of items you have rated in the most frequent three columns. If you see several of these, you may find it difficult to get through all of them on your own. This is another indication that some professional assistance might be very helpful to you in reducing the frequency of your unproductive feelings and behaviors and coping with your life in general.

Now, consider the items you rated as "Almost never" or "Never." With the exception of the items marked with (**) as noted above, these items are probably giving you little or no trouble at all. You probably have little need for professional counseling for these issues at this time. As time passes, and your healing process continues, you should find more and more of your troubling feelings and behaviors moving over into the "Never" column (see below for instructions on repeating this exercise a month from now).

Finally, remember, *if you score low on this scale, but feel a need for some professional help nonetheless, follow your instincts.*

OK, the exercise is repeated below. Wait about 1 month and complete the checklist again.

SELF-EXPLORATION
Do You Need Professional Help? (II): 1 month later

After at least a month has passed from the first time, complete this self-exploration again. Take your time as you go through this checklist. Be honest with yourself. You will only be hurting yourself by fudging the answers.

The more frequent the feelings and behaviors and the more checks you see when you are done, the greater the potential benefits from counseling. (**Note**: If you are having any suicidal thoughts, you should seek professional help immediately.)

If you decide to seek therapy, you can also complete this exercise anytime during your counseling process for a clear assessment of your progress.

Behavior as of _____ (date)	Check the frequency of your behavior				
	Very often	Often	Once in a while	Almost never	Never
Angry verbal outbursts	_____	_____	_____	_____	_____
Feeling enraged	_____	_____	_____	_____	_____
Throwing things	_____	_____	_____	_____	_____
Hitting things	_____	_____	_____	_____	_____
Hitting people or animals**	_____	_____	_____	_____	_____
Feeling hopeless	_____	_____	_____	_____	_____
Feeling helpless	_____	_____	_____	_____	_____
Changes in sleeping	_____	_____	_____	_____	_____
Changes in eating	_____	_____	_____	_____	_____
Feeling sad and "blue"	_____	_____	_____	_____	_____
Thoughts of self-injury	_____	_____	_____	_____	_____
Self-injurious actions**	_____	_____	_____	_____	_____
Suicide attempts**	_____	_____	_____	_____	_____

Behavior as of _____(date)	Very often	Often	Once in a while	Almost never	Never
Suicidal thoughts**	_____	_____	_____	_____	_____
Excessive worrying	_____	_____	_____	_____	_____
Headaches	_____	_____	_____	_____	_____
Stomach problems	_____	_____	_____	_____	_____
Neck aches	_____	_____	_____	_____	_____
Backaches	_____	_____	_____	_____	_____
Anxiety	_____	_____	_____	_____	_____
Panic attacks	_____	_____	_____	_____	_____
Other	_____	_____	_____	_____	_____
Other	_____	_____	_____	_____	_____

Important note: As before, if the items marked (**) are checked in any column except "Never," you should seek counseling immediately, regardless of your overall score on this exercise.

Interpreting Your Ratings:

Compare your scores this time with your results from a month ago. You should see the overall frequency of your troubling feelings and behaviors decreasing. That is, you should see the behaviors you rated as "Very often" or "Often" beginning to move down to the "Once in a while," "Almost never," or "Never" columns and more of the "Once in a while" or "Almost never" items now checked in the "Never" category.

If you do not see any improvement, or your painful feelings and behaviors are becoming *more* frequent, this may be an important sign for you to seek out or to continue some professional counseling. Some therapy with a therapist trained in abuse issues can help you to move past these issues and continue on your path of healing.

Finally, as we said a month ago, *if you score low on this scale, but feel a need for some professional help nonetheless, follow your instincts.*

14

Believing in Yourself

For so long I thought I deserved all the bad things that were happening to me. People tell me all the time I deserve better, but I still have a hard time believing it.

ANNE, AGE 57

I got so little for so long. Why should I believe that it's going to be any different now?

PHYLLIS, AGE 72

In my head I know I didn't deserve that kind of treatment. But I'm not sure I really believe it in my gut.

JERRI, AGE 22

Myth: After an abusive relationship, your self-esteem has nowhere to go but up.

Myth: Believing in yourself is easy when you are free from your abuser.

Myth: People have very little control over their self-esteem.

Assessing Your Self-Concept

How would you describe yourself to a stranger, someone you've never met and who knows nothing about you? Think how you would answer if the stranger asked you to be as detailed as possible and include both the positive and negative in your self-description? Which list would be longer, your pluses or your minuses?

As silly as this question sounds, it's a way to begin to assess your current level of self-esteem. Self-esteem is complicated. It embodies many ingredients that make up how you judge yourself. Do you like who you are? Do you believe you deserve the best from life? Or do you feel unworthy of life's gifts? Healthy self-esteem implies that you see yourself as a person who has as much right to happiness and satisfaction in life as anyone else.

If you have not paid attention to your self-esteem, it may be time to start. Make a list of your unique, healthy, and positive attributes. Include all the qualities that make you a good person and the traits you especially like about yourself. Your list might include central self-concepts such as honesty, your sense of humor, your trusting nature, or your sensitivity to the feelings of others. It should also contain those more outward characteristics such as your laugh, the shape of your nose, or the way you dance.

Did you find it difficult to complete your list? If you are like most survivors of abuse, you haven't spent much time thinking about your good qualities. While you were in that relationship, it may have been no time at all. All too often, survivors of abusive relationships forget completely how wonderful they are.

Was it uncomfortable for you to list your positives? Did you feel embarrassed, afraid someone might see it and think you terribly vain? Believing in yourself does not mean you are conceited or arrogant. It means you like yourself, that's all, and that's good.

Who You Were before the Abuse

It's not always true that your life would be terrific if only you hadn't suffered through that relationship. Is it possible your life was not exactly perfect before the abuse?

As you begin to heal and change your life, considering when your current difficulties began is important. How did you feel about yourself before your abusive relationship? Were you a confident, self-assured individual with a positive and healthy self-concept? Did you see yourself as a good friend, a good partner, a loving parent, and a productive worker? How much time did you spend taking care of yourself and *your* needs versus taking care of others? Were you as good to yourself as to everyone else in your life? Or was it easier to care for others and neglect yourself?

Your self-esteem may have been healthy before the relationship, and it was the abuse that caused you to lose faith in yourself. On the other hand, you may have had a less-than-positive self-image long before the abuse. For some survivors, self-esteem and self-confidence problems didn't begin with the abuse; the abuse only made them worse. Many people suffer from low self-esteem, and, often, the causes are unclear. A person's upbringing, family dynamics, culture, friends, and peers all play a significant role in his or her self-concept as an adult. So in your process of becoming a fully functioning person, it will help to recognize any past influences you may need to work on as you heal from the abuse.

Those Critical Voices in Your Head

Do you ever feel as though little voices inside your head are saying you are not good enough? Maybe a voice says, "Who are you to think that you can . . ." or "Oh, sure, like *you* could ever succeed at . . . ?" Have you tried to figure out whose voice it is? Maybe it's time to do that.

The next time you sense one of those belittling or degrading voices, think about who said those kinds of words to you. You will probably think of your abuser first, but were there others in your past as well? Who made you feel you were not good enough? Who came up with negative comments no matter what you did or how hard you tried? Who reacted to your accomplishments with silence: no criticisms, but no compliments or praise? Did someone offer support in certain ways but in other areas constantly put you down? Who was it that picked apart the way you looked?

Your abuser probably embodied all these people. Looking back on his insults and humiliations, it's easy to see how he made you lose faith in yourself. To keep you, he probably broke your spirit and made you feel unworthy. Destroying your self-esteem was a very powerful strategy for controlling you.

However, long before he came onto the scene, maybe others set the stage for your poor self-esteem. Now, in the process of learning to love yourself and becoming a strong, self-assured person, looking at all these influences is essential.

Hearing Your Abuser's Voice

Throughout this book we have been talking about ways your abuser's behavior was designed, in part, to destroy your self-esteem. It's imperative for you to remind yourself frequently why he said what he did. All the verbal, psychological, and physical abuse was calculated to control you. If he could convince you of your unworthiness, his hold over you was strengthened. And he was good at it. He knew exactly which buttons to push. He would identify your most insecure areas, where your self-esteem was already a little shaky, and zero in on them. However, all those insulting and degrading comments were not really about you. They were about him and his pathological need for control.

Realizing and remembering the true purpose of his put-downs and slurs is essential for healing. Every time you hear his voice in your head, remind yourself his words were totally unjustified. Even if you see a grain of truth in some of his comments, keep in mind he was exaggerating them, using them as a weapon, and manipulating them to his own ends. For example, your abuser may have set up impossible expectations and when you could not or would not meet them, he would accuse you of being unreliable and untrustworthy. It was his problem, not yours. However, now that you are out and no longer controlled by him, you may still see yourself as thoughtless or undependable. If so, that's his voice still exerting some control over you.

The truth is that no one is perfect and it's unfair to expect perfection of yourself, even if your abuser expected it of you. You may *want* to change some aspects of yourself, and that's healthy. Everyone has characteristics or behaviors they would like to change. But just because you want to change does not mean you are not a great person right now.

When It's Not Your Abuser's Voice

If the derogatory voice running through your mind belongs to someone from a time before the abusive relationship (such as a parent, father, an older sibling, a friend, etc.), you may need to pay attention to it. Anyone who diminished your self-esteem while you were growing up may have created a difficult and long-lasting burden.

Recognizing that someone from your past helped to create your negative self-concepts does not mean you now have to hate, blame, or confront that person. What it means is you need to work through those issues.

It is very painful to discover that a friend or family member undermined your self-esteem. Even if they had no intention of causing you to think less of yourself, they did just that. Many reasons may be found to explain why friends or family members are not always supportive and encouraging. Usually, they don't realize the impact of their words and actions. They may have thought they were making you a stronger person by telling you the truth as they saw it. Maybe they were treating you as they were treated when growing up. Whatever the reason, you need to consider all these factors in the work you are doing to heal from the abuse.

Perhaps you are feeling influenced by voices, other than his, from the time *during* the abuse. Maybe you still hear the echoes of those people who tried to tell you, directly or indirectly, the abuse was your fault or you were nuts to stay as long as you did. Many reasons for their actions are discussed in chapter 11, "The Reaction of Others." Their opinions and comments were probably due to ignorance of abusive relationships or the fact that the charming facade of your abuser deceived them. Keeping their comments in proper perspective can help you to let go of them. They were not seeing the truth of your life.

Purging the Voices from Your Past

Looking back, it's not always easy to recognize why a friend or family member treated you so poorly. If you could find some understandable reason, letting go of the negative beliefs they caused might be easier. But if no explanation surfaces, you may feel as if their voices will haunt you forever.

Usually, ridding yourself of the voices from the past involves recognizing the harmful thoughts and working to change them. You will need time to place those voices in their proper perspective. Once you understand the true motives behind the voices, remind yourself often that the words are false. You need not allow them to cause you pain any longer. Reviewing the discussion on "thought stopping" in chapter 9, "Managing Your Stress," will also help you silence the voices.

Talking with trusted members of your family or others who were with you when these old relationships existed may also be very helpful (see the self-awareness exercise at the end of this chapter). Discuss with them your perception of what happened back then and how you felt. You may hear something such as "I know exactly what you mean, I felt the same thing!" Knowing you were not alone then and are not alone now can be wonderfully comforting. You may also find that others can give you new insight into those past events. This new knowledge may accelerate the process of eliminating the old, painful voices.

If nothing works and the preabuse voices continue to affect your self-image, it may be time to seek some professional help to silence them once and for all (see chapter 13, "Beginning to Heal").

When the Voice Is Yours

Sometimes if someone else puts you down, insults, and degrades you for long enough, you begin to believe it's true. The controlling judgments begin to eat away at your self-image. Over time, his voice evolves into yours. He may be gone, his voice may have faded, but you still hear his words in your voice. When this happens, destructive comments have the greatest power over you. If the critical voice is yours, it may take some extra time and work for you to unlearn these unhealthy beliefs.

Have you assumed your abuser's role of belittling yourself? Do you treat yourself, as he did, with less respect and caring than you deserve? If so, it's time to begin to treat *yourself* with dignity and appreciation.

Letting Go and Opening Up

Change is difficult, even if it is for the better. Knowing you deserve to feel better about yourself will not, by itself, cause it to happen. You must have patience and give yourself time. Letting go of negative ideas about yourself can be frightening. It creates the possibility of unknown feelings and new self-expectations. Remember, no one expects you to be perfect. So you need not expect perfection of yourself. Try to see yourself as a worthy and deserving person, even if, like everyone, you are not the best at everything you attempt. Just allow yourself to be human as you rediscover who you really are.

SELF-EXPLORATION
Who Are You? (I)

The first step toward increasing your self-esteem is rediscovering who you really are. The following exercise is designed to help you look at your character, personality, values, and overall human qualities. Mark each of the following items that you believe describes you. Add as many additional positive characteristics as you can. Fill out each section in as much detail as possible. If you find that you get stuck in a particular area, leave it blank for now, but keep it in mind over the next week or so. As you go about your daily life, try to uncover your positive characteristics that fit into that category.

As in some previous chapters, you will notice two copies of this exercise are included. Fill out the first copy this week and the second copy 1 month from now. After you have completed the exercise for the second time, compare the two lists. If your lists are similar and are lacking in positive attributes in any category, you still have work to do on your self-esteem. If, on the other hand, your second list contains a lot more positive qualities, you are heading in the right direction as you reclaim your self-confidence and self-esteem.

Professional skills (hard worker, conscientious, dedicated, team player, etc.) _____

_____

_____

_____

_____

_____

_____

_____

_____

_____

_____

Interpersonal skills (good listener, communicates thoughts and feelings well, giving, etc.) _____

_____

_____

_____

_____

_____

_____

_____

Intelligence and common sense _____

_____

_____

_____

_____

_____

_____

_____

Values and ethics (honest, trustworthy, spiritual, etc.) _____

_____

_____

_____

_____

_____

_____

_____

Positive outlook (optimistic, upbeat, sense of humor, etc.) _____

_____

_____

_____

_____

_____

_____

_____

_____

_____

Yourself in relation to the world (environmentally conscious, kind to animals, concerned about others, etc.) _____

_____

_____

_____

_____

_____

_____

_____

_____

Other _____

_____

_____

_____

_____

_____

_____

_____

Who Are You? (II): 1 month later

Professional skills (hard worker, conscientious, dedicated, team player, etc.) _____

_____

_____

_____

_____

_____

_____

_____

_____

_____

Interpersonal skills (good listener, communicates thoughts and feelings well, giving, etc.) _____

_____

_____

_____

_____

_____

_____

_____

Intelligence and common sense _____

_____

_____

_____

_____

_____

_____

_____

_____

_____

Values and ethics (honest, trustworthy, spiritual, etc.) _____

_____

_____

_____

_____

_____

_____

_____

_____

Positive outlook (optimistic, upbeat, sense of humor, etc.) _____

_____

_____

_____

_____

_____

_____

_____

Yourself in relation to the world (environmentally conscious, kind
to animals, concerned about others, etc.) _____

_____

_____

_____

_____

_____

_____

_____

_____

_____

Other _____

_____

_____

_____

_____

_____

_____

_____

Now compare your self-assessment to the one you did a month or so ago. Analyze the changes you see, if any, over the past 4 weeks. If your list hasn't changed much and still seems too skimpy on positives in any category, you still have work to do on your self-esteem. If, on the other hand, your second list contains more positive qualities, in all or most categories, you are heading in the right direction as you heal your self-confidence and self-esteem.

15

The Temptation to Go Back

My family thought I was crazy when I said I was thinking about going back to him. They were angry. They even stopped talking to me.

ANA, AGE 41

One minute I think I'm a masochist to consider going back and the next minute I'm thinking about how funny and smart he is. Sometimes I really miss him.

ELAINE, AGE 55

Myth: Once a woman is out of an abusive relationship, she would never consider returning to her abuser.

Myth: Any woman who returns to an abusive partner is weak and probably cannot survive on her own.

Myth: If a battered woman leaves her abuser and then goes back to him, any further abuse she suffers is her fault.

Note: You know how difficult it was for you to leave your abuser. You know all the reasons you left: fear, humiliation, loss of self-esteem, isolation, physical danger, and so on. For all those reasons you changed your life and escaped from his control. Ultimately, only you can decide whether to go back. Should you ever find yourself considering returning to that relationship, this chapter is designed to help you make an informed, mindful decision. It is by no means a recommendation that you go back. Rather, it is saying that if you ever do decide to go back, here is some advice you may need.

Anyone who has not endured an abusive relationship may find it very difficult to understand how you could ever consider, even for a moment, returning to your abuser. If you are contemplating returning and have attempted to discuss it with friends or family, they probably reacted with shock, disbelief, anger, and recriminations. Ironically, you may find yourself in the position of having only your former abuser to confide in about this difficult decision.

Some women become very upset with themselves at the thought of returning to their abusive relationship. They ask themselves if they are crazy to contemplate such a seemingly irrational act.

As we have discussed frequently in this book, reconstructing your life after an abusive relationship is never easy. Your new existence contains so many new sources of stress, apprehension, and doubt. You feel a very real sense of loss. Sometimes, you may feel as if you were happier with him than without him. Missing the positive aspects of your life with him is completely understandable. The awful, painful, and traumatic events in your relationship may not completely erase the good times. And every now and then it may seem easier to just go back.

Feelings such as these do not by any means obligate you to return. They are a normal part of the recovery process. However, you must weigh the pros and cons of returning and decide your best course of action. It's OK to *think* about it. You are in control of your life now, and it's up to you to make the best choices for your life.

Weighing the Pros and Cons

As with any major decision, you need to examine your options thoroughly. Pencil and paper can be very helpful in these difficult decisions. List all the pros and cons of going back and all the pros and cons of staying away. When you look at your lists, deciding may be easier for you.

Begin by writing the positive characteristics of the relationship such as financial security, companionship, having an intimate partner, owning a home, and so on. Next, write down your ex-partner's positive traits such as, perhaps, his sense of humor, interests you shared, his physical appearance, or any other characteristics you liked. Take your time with these lists. Do not hurry through them. If you need to, write a little, put them away for a while, then go back and add additional items later. You need not rush through it.

When you have your list of the positive factors, move on to the next list: the negatives. List all the painful, humiliating, frightening, and traumatic events during your time with your abuser. Include the basic human needs and desires such as respect, emotional security, trust, or a violence-free life that were lacking in that relationship. Record all the factors that made you want to leave.

Your next task will be to write all of the negative personal characteristics of your former partner. Try to concentrate on the attributes that were damaging or harmful to you then and probably would be again if you go back. Items on this list might include his irrational jealousy, his way of treating you as his property, his controlling behaviors, or his violence.

Making these pro and con lists may understandably be painful for you. Keep reminding yourself that you are out now. It is completely your decision to go back to him or not. No one else can tell you what is best for you.

After you have finished your lists, tally up all the pros and cons. What do you see? Is the number of pros and cons about equal or did one side far outweigh the other? Before you seriously consider making another major change in your life, review these lists carefully. Deciding impulsively and without thorough deliberation would be a mistake.

If you struggle repeatedly with ideas of returning, your pro and con lists may come in handy more than once. Each time you are considering going back, you can review them and add or subtract items.

Remembering Why You Left

Another way to decide if you should return is to reconsider why you left in the first place (see the self-exploration exercise at the end of this chapter). You left because you were being abused. You left because you were afraid. You left because your life and your dignity had been taken from you. Remember the terrible difficulty getting out? Remember how long it took?

You may believe things would be different with him now. He may be telling you how much he has changed. Reviewing the reasons you left will help remind you of your life with him. Before you decide to return, you need to be sure you will not be stepping back into the same old abusive pattern.

Remembering the Cycle

One all-too-familiar element in your relationship was the cycle of abuse. This repeating sequence of "honeymoon, tension-building, explosion" was an ingrained part of your relationship (see chapter 1, "Were You in an Abusive Relationship?"). You knew the good times would always be followed, eventually, by the bad times. You also knew once the tension began to mount, there was no going back. The abuse would come.

This cycle of abuse is extremely difficult to break. Unless your ex-abuser is participating in ongoing therapy specifically designed to deal with his abusive nature, the cycle will resurface. Rarely does the cycle end on its own. Even with effective treatment, an abuser will need time and a deep commitment to change. Unfortunately, many abusers are never able to break the cycle.

Treatment for the Abuser

Very specific treatment has been developed for men who are abusive. *Couples therapy* (sometimes referred to as marriage counseling) is **not** recommended and can be dangerous for a couple with one controlling and abusive partner. Sitting next to her abuser, a woman often feels intimidated and afraid to be honest about the real problems in the relationship. Frequently this may cause the therapist to be unaware of the seriousness of the abuse or, at times, unknowingly side with the abuser. If the woman dares to mention the abuse, her abuser later punishes her. Therefore, couples therapy can create conditions that result in more frequent and escalating abuse.

Most professionals agree the only effective treatment for abusers is that referred to as *batterers' treatment groups*. These groups force the abuser to examine his belief systems about women and relationships and to face head-on his violent behavior as well as the roots of his violence.

For an abuser simply to begin a batterers' treatment group is not enough. Before he has a chance of establishing a healthy, loving relationship, he must *complete* the entire treatment program. Even then, no one can guarantee he will be able to remain abuse-free, especially with the woman who was the target of his abuse. Even with the best treatment, your abuser may return to his controlling, abusive, or violent behaviors.

Therefore, if your ex-partner seeks treatment or seems to be getting better, you must be very careful and vigilant to be sure this is true. As you may well know, abusers are experts in subtle forms of manipulation and deception. His abusive tendencies may not be gone at all. Instead, he may just have found new techniques for concealing them. If you think he has changed and you are considering going back, look for the most subtle signs. Now he may not become physically violent, but may rely on less obvious abusive tactics. Instead of throwing objects or striking you, he just makes a fist. You know what that fist means, and falling right into old patterns of fear and control, you do exactly what he wants. That same sickening knot in your gut comes back.

If your abuser claims to have changed, you should be cautious if he avoids situations or discussions that set him off in the past. Complete avoidance of these "hot button" issues suggests he has not worked through them. He is simply avoiding them for now, but eventually they are likely to reignite his abuse.

If alcohol or other drug use by your partner was part of the abuse in any way, this is another factor for you to consider. As we have said elsewhere in this book, alcohol or other drugs do not *cause* relationship abuse or violence, but they often contribute to and intensify it. Also, don't forget how often he tried to excuse his behavior by blaming it on alcohol or other drugs. If your former partner is still using alcohol or other drugs, the potential is very strong for even worse abuse in the future if you go back. If your abuser says he has stopped using alcohol or other drugs and is sober now, do not assume that this signals the end or even a reduction of his abusive behaviors.

Finally, listen to your gut and heart. If your interactions with him produce the slightest decrease in your self-esteem, your sense of independence, or your feelings of safety, be cautious in deciding to return to that relationship.

Remember How Far You've Come

If you are thinking about going back to your abuser, what are some signs that you are ready to return to that relationship? Just as you need to go back with a full awareness of your partner's potential behavior, you may also benefit from looking at how much you've changed since leaving him. This will help you decide if going back is worth the possibility of losing all that you have gained during your healing process. It will also help you determine the personal strengths and characteristics you will need to be able to return to that relationship as safely as possible

Think back to all the reasons it was so difficult for you to leave him. Remember all of his excuses, accusations, and manipulations. Do you feel you would be able this time to stand up to those behaviors should they happen again? What is different about you now? If you ever consider going back you must be sure that your self-esteem, self-confidence, sense of personal security, and inner strength are powerful enough to allow you to escape the relationship again.

How have you dealt with the hurt, anger, fear, and other emotions? Walking back into any relationship in which you have unresolved negative feelings is setting yourself up for a difficult time.

Most likely, those unresolved feelings will not heal when you are back in the relationship if they failed to heal while you were apart.

If you have been struggling with a problem with alcohol or other drugs, you may want to conquer this concern before you return to your former partner. If you return, you will need all your faculties at their sharpest to be fully tuned in to your surroundings. Alcohol and other drugs dull your perception and make it more difficult for you to see all the nuances and possible danger signs of your partner's behavior and the relationship itself.

Although only you can decide if it is in your best interest to return to that previously abusive relationship, you may want to talk your decision over with a trusted friend, family member, or therapist. Chose someone who will help you consider all sides and be honest with you about their insights, but not try to control your decision. If you are considering going back, you should be sure you perceive yourself as a confident, self-assured person who knows how much she deserves and will not settle for less.

Deciding Not to Go Back

If you decide not to go back, do not waste your time worrying about why you even considered it. Feeling tempted to return to your abuser is a common and normal stage in the healing process. It does not suggest you are weak or there is something psychologically wrong with you.

When these thoughts of returning appear, and they may from time to time, get out your lists of pros and cons. Remind yourself it's OK to remember and miss the good things, but be sure you don't overlook the negatives.

Seek the support of friends. Tell them how they can help when you are in one of your "going back" phases. If reminding you of all the reasons you left will help, ask them to do that. If you simply need them to listen, tell them that too.

Also, you could try reversing the roles. Look at yourself from another angle. What if someone you care deeply about was in the same situation? Imagine how you would feel if your best friend or your sister managed to find her way out of an abusive relationship such as yours and is now considering whether to go back to her abuser. What would you think? How would you advise her if she asked for your help? Would you suggest that going back to him would be likely to make her happy? This imaginary scenario may help you have confidence in your decision. Whatever you choose to do, make sure your decisions are based on what is in your best interests. You deserve to have a loving, respectful, and safe intimate relationship.

If You Decide to Go Back

If you decide to return to your ex-partner, be sure to do so with your eyes wide open. Know ahead of time, no matter what he is saying now, he may, sooner or later, return to his old abusive ways. If he has not completed a batterers' treatment program, you may want to make his full completion of such a program a requirement for any discussion of reconciliation. If he is desperate and manipulative in his desire to get you back, he may lie about his participation in the program. Therefore, you need to arrange for the therapist who facilitates the batterers' group to report his attendance and progress to you directly.

If you are considering returning, establish your requirements and limits *now*. Decide what you must have from a relationship and what you will not accept—and stick to it. Drawing these lines early should help you take quick action to protect yourself if the relationship deteriorates into abuse and violence again.

Make an action plan. With a plan in place, you will be more likely to stay safely out of danger if you feel his abusive behaviors surfacing.

Be sure to keep close tabs on how you are feeling. Look for indicators of depression and any decrease in your self-esteem (see chapter 8, "Signs of Unfinished Healing"). If you begin to feel these familiar responses, think of them as warnings of possible trouble ahead.

If you decide to go back, think about how you will deal with others in your life. Having an effective support network and people close to you whom you trust will be vitally important. Even if they do not agree with your decision, let them know you honestly feel it is the right one, you have considered it carefully, and you will continue to need them in your life.

Some of the supportive people in your life may feel very frightened for your well-being, feel you are making the wrong decision, or even feel betrayed after they tried to help you. You may find them backing away from you. Try to keep the lines of communication open with them. Do not allow yourself to become isolated and totally dependent on your partner once again.

Considering Your Options

In trying to decide whether to go back to an abusive relationship, some specific guidelines can be helpful. The chart below will help you look at various aspects of your relationship. For each personality characteristic or behavior, mark where you believe your ex-partner would fall on the scale.

Factors in the Relationship and Your Ex-Partner

Trusting	__ __ __ __ __ __ __ __ __ __	Suspicious
Respectful	__ __ __ __ __ __ __ __ __ __	Contemptuous
Predictable	__ __ __ __ __ __ __ __ __ __	Unpredictable
Liberating	__ __ __ __ __ __ __ __ __ __	Possessive
Egalitarian	__ __ __ __ __ __ __ __ __ __	Controlling
Secure	__ __ __ __ __ __ __ __ __ __	Jealous
Good parent	__ __ __ __ __ __ __ __ __ __	Unhealthy role model
Dependable	__ __ __ __ __ __ __ __ __ __	Undependable
Stable	__ __ __ __ __ __ __ __ __ __	Unstable
Empowering	__ __ __ __ __ __ __ __ __ __	Demeaning
Willing to change	__ __ __ __ __ __ __ __ __ __	Denies he has a problem

This information combined with your responses to the self-exploration in chapter 1, "Were You in an Abusive Relationship?", will provide a helpful foundation for deciding whether or not to return to your abuser.

16

Is He Still in Your Life?

Once I left, I thought that was it. I thought he was gone forever. I can't believe I still have to see him so often.

JULIE, AGE 47

I see him all the time. I have no choice. So how can I possibly get on with my life?

MARILYN, AGE 54

Every time I see him, I get so upset. I see him at parties and he's in one of my classes. I just want him to go away.

KEISHA, AGE 20

Myth: Once you leave an abusive relationship, you are free from any interactions with your abuser.

Myth: Following an abusive relationship you have control over all contacts with your ex-partner.

Myth: Now that you are out, there is no way for him to exert any control over you.

No matter how much you would like to exclude your ex-partner from your life, it is not always possible to do so. Your abuser may continue to be a part of your current life in many ways, and contact with him may be unavoidable, especially if you have children together. Therefore, developing effective strategies to deal with him is a vital component in your healing process.

Contact with Him at Work or in the Community

If you and your abuser are still living in the same community, you may have no choice about seeing him. If you work in the same location, you may have to interact on a frequent or even daily basis. Getting on with your life may be a bit more difficult under these conditions.

Even if you are unable to avoid contact, you should be able to decline to interact with him. No matter what he says or does, you have every right to insist that he refrain from talking or interacting with you in any way. If he refuses to comply with your wishes, you may need to consider a restraining order (see chapter 12, "Practical Considerations").

If your abuser knows where you work and live, it becomes even more imperative that you examine your personal safety needs. Review chapter 2, "Are You Out Of Danger Now?", and take all necessary steps to maximize your safety.

If he attempts any contact while a restraining order is in force, call the police immediately. Don't wait for the situation to get out of hand. The easiest way to keep him out of your life is to demonstrate clearly that you will not be controlled again. This time you are the one in control. Every situation is unique, but if possible, it is wise for you to avoid ever initiating contact with him. If you do this or respond to his overtures in any way, you may be allowing him to get a "foot in the door."

Indirect Contact through Family and Friends

Your abuser may reappear in your life through your family and friends. Remember how charming others thought he was? Remember how he fooled people into thinking he was such a wonderful partner? He still has those talents. Now that you have left, he may be desperate to get you back. He is more dangerous than ever before. He will try everything possible to recapture you, including using the people who are still in your life.

If he has contact with your family and friends, you should expect he will try to win their approval and enlist their help. He will say he has changed, the children need him, he has been getting help, and he will do anything for you. He will tell them it will never happen again.

Remember how much *you* wanted to believe him when he said these things? Your loved ones may feel the same. This will be particularly true if they know you are struggling and having a difficult time on your own. They will be looking for a storybook ending. In their desire to make you happy, they may be fooled by his overtures.

You will need to be understanding but firm with your friends and family. Let them know you appreciate how much they care. Let them know you are very aware of how convincing he can be. Then, try to help them see his deceptive ways and why you are choosing not to return to an abusive man.

Unwanted Contacts with "His Camp"

You may also find that his family and friends will contact you. They will be acting on his behalf, working to convince you he is sorry and what a great guy he is. You need to be prepared to respond effectively to these contacts.

Those who see or talk to him on an ongoing basis probably do not fully understand what happened in your relationship. At this point, trying to enlighten them will probably be futile.

If they contact you, the best approach is to tell them in very clear language how you feel and what you will and will not do. Do not argue with them. Do not try to reason with them. Just let them know your limits.

Keep in mind whatever you tell them will be passed along to your ex-partner. So be careful about how much you say. You do not need to explain or defend your decisions. You simply need to inform them of what you want and expect, not only from him but from them as well. If you want no further contact with them, tell them so. Again, be clear and firm.

Contact through the Children

One of the most common reasons a woman must have contact with her ex-partner involves children. If you and your ex-partner had children together, he may have visitation rights (see chapter 10, "What About the Children?"). Another possibility is that you may have been forced to leave your children with him when you escaped. Seeing your children now may necessitate seeing your abuser as well.

If your ex-partner has visitation rights, it will be important for you to plan visits that will be as safe as possible for you and your children. Some cities and towns provide *visitation centers*, which allow visits between parents and children in safe, supervised settings. If visitation centers are available in your area seriously consider using them. Contact your local sexual assault and domestic violence crisis center for information about visitation centers in your area. Be sure to read chapter 10, "What About the Children?", for additional information on visitation safety.

Hearing About Him from the Children

Even if you do not have direct contact with your ex-partner, you still may hear about him. If your children see him, they're bound to tell you about their visits. As painful as that may be for you, it will more painful to forbid your kids to talk about their father. That just puts *them* in the middle, which may be exactly what your ex-partner wants.

From a distance, your abuser can attempt to influence and control you in many ways. One route is through your children. He may plant stories and comments he knows they will convey to you. It's important for you to anticipate his manipulations of the children. The more prepared you are for his indirect maneuvers, the easier it will be for you to deal with them when they occur.

You may believe your abuser would never hurt your children, because all his abuse was directed at you. Sadly, after the relationship ends, an abuser may employ new tactics to control you, including abusive acts directed at your children. You need to be extremely cautious about your children's safety.

If your ex-partner has contact with your children through a visitation center, be sure you clearly understand the rules of that center. There will be a very strict set of regulations he will have to obey. These rules will prohibit all violence or threats of violence toward you or your children. They will also prevent your abuser from determining through them where you are living or gaining access to you in any way. The trained staff should help ensure he does not use the children to hurt you further.

If he breaks these rules, be sure to contact someone at the center immediately. Do not pass it off as a small transgression and let it go. If he gets away with one infraction, he will continue to push the limits. Remember, he wants to control your life and you need to undermine his efforts at every possible turn.

When He Lies to the Children

He might try to control you by lying to the children. He may work to convince them that you are the reason the family is not together or that you were cruel to him. He might fabricate whatever lies he thinks will turn the children against you. Hearing your children repeat these lies can have a profound emotional effect on you. Your children may frame the lies as questions to you, or they may say them as statements of fact. If they are posed as questions, try to respond without anger and resist your temptation to inhibit their desire for answers. If you are not able to respond calmly, just tell them you are glad they asked you and you will talk to them about it later. Be sure to keep that promise.

When you talk with your children, remember they are being used and placed in the middle by your abuser. They are trying to understand a very confusing situation. They may love their father, and he has said you hurt him. By asking you about it, they are trusting you to accept their confusion and help them understand. Try to be reassuring and nonaccusatory. It may help to tell them you know their father is sad and misses them very much. Be willing to listen as they tell you how hurt and upset he is. Acknowledge how unsettling it must be for them to hear this from him. You also need to tell them you have no choice. You cannot live with him anymore, and even though they may not understand it right now, you cannot do anything to make their father feel better.

Encourage them to come to you whenever they are confused or have questions. Let them know you will always love them no matter what they say or ask. Make sure they know they are not to blame for what happened between you and their father.

Manipulating the Children's Past and Future

Another way your abuser can control you is by trying to alter the children's memory of what actually happened. He might tell them you were the one who was abusive, not him. He might say he never hurt you or them or, if he did, it was only out of love. He might try to brainwash them the way he tried to brainwash you. You know how good he was at it.

Your former partner may tell the children you will be together again as a family one day. He may even say that if only you would give in and let him come home, you could all be happy. He may try anything to turn the children against you or to use them to regain control over you.

Using the Children to Control Your Activities

Another way your former abuser may exert control over you is by manipulating your schedule through the children. He may "play games" about when, where, and how he is going to see them. He could inconvenience you as much as possible to accommodate his visitation privileges. He may also use the children as a weapon, threatening to refuse to see them if you don't do what he wants.

Recognize this attempt to control you again. Do not let him use the children as another weapon against you. If he uses the children in this way, you have to ask yourself whether he should be with them at all. If he threatens that he will not see them unless you submit to his manipulations, losing touch with his children will be his decision, not yours.

Refuse to Be Controlled by Him

It can be extremely frustrating that he is still in your life. It took incredible courage and energy to leave. Now it may feel you will never get rid of him. You need to decide now what role, if any, you will allow him to play in your life. If you decide there is no place for him, try not to allow his contacting you, directly or indirectly, to exert control over you again. If you cannot find the strength within yourself for this, enlist the help of police, friends, or family. Seeking help is not a sign of weakness. You are dealing with a very difficult situation and a dangerous person.

Planning Ahead for Contact

What will you do when your abuser confronts you? It's a good idea to think about it now, so when it happens, you will be as prepared and in control as possible. The exercise below contains situations in which you may have contact with your ex-partner. Check all the ones you either know or think will apply to you. Then, in the space provided, indicate your best and most effective courses of action in that situation. You can always come back to this exercise and change your plans as needed.

Contact situation   *Action plan*

He shows up where I work:

_____

_____

_____

_____

_____

_____

I run into him at the market:

_____

_____

_____

_____

_____

He comes to my residence:

_____

_____

_____

_____

_____

Contact situation   *Action plan*

Our paths cross at a family function:

_____
_____
_____
_____
_____

We see each other at work:

_____
_____
_____
_____
_____

He is at my friend's house when I come to visit:

_____
_____
_____
_____
_____

We are both at the same restaurant:

_____
_____
_____
_____
_____

Other likely contact situations:

_____
_____
_____
_____
_____

17

Loving Again

I'm afraid to get involved with someone new. I just can't risk going through that again.

JENNIFER, AGE 30

Every time I get close to someone, that little voice inside my head tells me to pull back. I don't think I will ever be able to trust someone again.

ANITA, AGE 37

Guys keep asking me out and I keep saying no. I can't even bring myself to go to the off-campus parties I get invited to.

ALLIE, AGE 20

Myth: Survivors of abusive relationships are doomed to repeat the cycle.

Myth: Surviving an abusive relationship makes you an expert in predicting whether a potential partner has controlling or violent tendencies.

Myth: Most survivors are never able to find a truly intimate, loving relationship.

As a survivor of an abusive relationship, you may find it very difficult to allow intimacy into your life again. You are no longer able to enter into a new relationship with innocence and trust. You now carry with you the knowledge and, more importantly, the wisdom, of how love can go terribly wrong. Your experience of abuse means you may enter any new relationship with great caution. This is perfectly normal and very smart.

Are You Doomed to Future Abuse?

Just because you were in an abusive relationship does not, by any means, suggest that you will have to endure others. If anything, you will be better prepared to see the warning signs of a future partner's potential for controlling and abusive behavior. You can use what you have learned the hard way to be in touch with any warning signs that might be present.

By now there should be no doubt in your mind you were not to blame for your past abusive relationship. You weren't stupid or blind or too trusting. He was expert at concealing his abusive and violent nature. You had no way of seeing through his external charm and attractiveness. Now that you have experienced and survived your terrible ordeal, you can look back on your relationship and become aware of the signs that predicted the abuse.

What Do You Want from a Relationship?

Only you can determine who is the right partner for you, who has the qualities to make you comfortable and happy. However, this may be easier said than done. It's important for you to be clear about what you want in a relationship in advance and to remind yourself of your requirements each time a new potential partner enters your life. The self-exploration exercise at the end of this chapter, What to Look For and What to Avoid, is designed to help you with this task.

Warning Signs of Abuse

When you first met your ex-partner, you weren't looking for warning signs of abuse. You weren't keeping your eyes wide open for words or actions that might offer clues to his true nature. You certainly weren't mentally recording words, gestures, and actions that tied your stomach into a knot.

Some abusers are so skilled at hiding their true selves that no one, no matter how informed and experienced, would be able to predict they are capable of such abusive and violent actions. Other abusers may give off such subtle signs that only someone trained to know what to look for would detect them.

So what are some of the subtle signs that you should keep on your "abuse radar" screen? Indicators fall into two categories: subtle negative precursors of abuse and, paradoxically, more obvious signs in the form of seemingly wonderful, charming behaviors that feel a bit exaggerated or over the top.

Too Much of a Good Thing

Abusers can appear to be gracious, giving, loving, and devoted partners. From the moment you meet, they are working overtime to charm, impress, and entice you into a relationship. There is no end to how wonderful they appear while courting you. But how can you tell if he is simply the virtuous, caring person you are looking for or a "wolf in sheep's clothing"?

There's an adage that it's wonderful for a man to place a woman on a pedestal and that is what every woman wants. Unfortunately, that pedestal can also be a warning sign. When he places you on a pedestal, you are transformed into his perfect image of a woman, without flaws, who will always do and be exactly what he wants. It's his pedestal, not yours.

He Says You Are Perfect

There is a real danger in being such an idol. No one is perfect, and this sets an expectation of an impossible standard to meet. If a potential partner seems to be re-creating you in such an image, it's important to determine exactly how he really feels. If he is simply saying you are wonderful and he loves you unconditionally, that is probably a positive sign. But if he is saying he sees you as perfect, that's potentially dangerous.

If you are concerned that he is expecting perfection, make sure from the outset he is aware of your imperfections. If you are not always on time, do not go overboard to appear more punctual than you are. If you are not the best housekeeper in the world, let him see your home as it usually is: less than immaculate.

If you fail to live up to his image of you, and he is not upset, angry, or critical, there is less reason to be concerned. However, if he becomes annoyed, makes judgmental comments or jokes, or attempts to blame you for disappointing him, red flags and sirens should go off in your mind.

He Is Nothing if Not Persistent

Another seductive characteristic that is often a danger sign is his extreme persistence. If you are hesitant to become involved with him, but he refuses to take no for an answer, be alert. It's one thing for a man to let you know he's very interested, but to pursue you nonstop, even when you are withdrawing and asking for space, is a very disturbing sign.

His troubling overenthusiasm may also be evident in his desire for the relationship to move forward too quickly. If you find that he expresses his desire for a commitment (exclusivity, living together, marriage) soon after meeting you, that is good reason to be very concerned. Consider why he wants or needs the relationship to proceed at such a frantic pace. Is it love, or is it intense jealousy, insecurity, or his desire for control showing already?

If the speed of his desire for commitment makes you uncomfortable, see what happens if you step on the brakes. If he truly loves you in a healthy way, he should want to respect your desires and needs. If you tell him you like him but want to slow things down, he should be able and willing to respect your wishes. He should allow you to be in control in this regard. This means agreeing to take it as slowly as you want without pressuring you to pick up the pace or ridiculing you about going so slowly.

Monopolizing You

You should also pay attention to the amount of time he wants to spend with you. In any new relationship there is a desire to get to know the other person and the excitement of exploring someone new runs high. So how can you tell the difference between a genuine desire for togetherness and early attempts to control you?

At the beginning of a new relationship, you may want to limit your time together to specific, planned activities. This sets clear limits. If your potential new partner shows up frequently unannounced and unplanned, you should be cautious. Tell him you prefer to arrange your time together. If he shows up at your job, explain that it is not a good time or place for you to meet. If he argues with you, or disregards your wishes about this, it might indicate a problem.

If he wants to spend every evening and all weekend together and calls you frequently in between, tell him you are not yet ready to become involved with anyone to that extent. Suggest that you see each other only a couple of nights per week. Let him know you have plans on other evenings and on the weekend and you need some time to yourself. Pay attention to his response and take his reactions into consideration. If he discounts or ignores your wishes, he is trying to control you already.

Jealousy

If he shows signs of jealousy on your first or second date, before you are even a couple, there is a clear problem. If you don't notice this early jealousy, but his possessiveness and expressions of ownership escalate as the relationship continues, keep an eye on it. If he becomes jealous without a reason, that should be a red flag. If his jealousy is out of proportion to your innocent interactions with others, that, too, is a reason for concern. He may say that his jealousy is the result of his intense attraction to you and how desirable other men are sure to find you. As flattering as that may feel, you need to recognize that excessive jealousy is about his insecurity and his need to control you. It is not about love and caring.

Isolating You

Isolating you from other people in your life is a very disturbing indication of future danger. If he always wants to be alone with you and resists spending time with your family and friends, he is beginning to isolate you already. Another sign of this control tactic is his tendency to manipulate you into canceling plans with others so that the two of you can be alone. Again, it may sound romantic, but a pattern of this behavior is not romantic, it's dangerous.

He's Not All That Bad

It's very important to keep an eye on those behaviors that annoy you but don't feel like true warning signs yet. Someone without your experience of abuse might easily dismiss them. Here are some examples.

Hints of the excessive jealousy we discussed earlier may begin with the feeling that he is checking up on you. It is a worrisome sign if he calls you too frequently at home or at work. These calls may include questions about your whereabouts or whom you were with at a specified time. He may find creative excuses for his persistent phone calls, or he may just attribute them to missing you.

Be very cautious if you find that he is following you. Although he may not make contact, you may see him driving by your home or workplace. When you are out with your friends, he may "coincidentally" show up at the same location. All of these are signs of his jealous and controlling nature that you should interpret as warning signs.

Does he try to make most of the decisions in your relationship, such as where you will go together and what you will do? If your desires differ, do his always seem to take priority? Does he find subtle little ways to discount and disparage the activities you choose? These are clear indicators of controlling tendencies.

Another sign of a need to dominate you involves jokes and subtle put-downs about you and issues that are important to you. This may take the form of demeaning teasing or joking about your personal idiosyncrasies such as being occasionally late, keeping a somewhat messy home, or driving cautiously. This warning sign may be more noticeable if he teases and jokes about you in the presence of others.

If you are unsure that these warning behaviors indicate trouble ahead, put them to the test. Confront the behaviors. Refuse to accept them. See if he makes the changes you desire and for how long. There is no rush. Trusting someone may take time, but it will be worth the wait to find someone who is truly right for you.

What Is a Healthy Relationship?

No two people want exactly the same qualities in an intimate relationship. Characteristics that are very significant to you may be less important to someone else. There are, however, some key elements of healthy relationships that all of us deserve from our partners.

Equality is very important. Equality doesn't imply that you and your partner are the same. It doesn't mean you both should share all the same activities such as fixing the car, doing the dishes, paying the bills, planting the garden. It means there is a sense of balance in your relationship. This applies to all activities from chores and work to an equal share in all family decisions.

Everyone deserves *respect* from an intimate partner. Respect should permeate all aspects of your relationship. It's not enough to respect someone for their looks, cooking abilities, or musical talent. You deserve to be respected for who you are as a person, outstanding characteristics, flaws, and all.

Trust is another crucial ingredient in all healthy relationships. It is essential to know you can rely on your partner. This means that your new partner should be honest and consistent. (You should never have to question the validity of what he is telling you. Above all else, you should be able to trust that there will never be any abuse or violence.)

Looking inside Yourself

How do you know if you are ready for a new relationship? Along with your careful analysis of a potential new relationship, it will be helpful for you to evaluate your own readiness to become romantically involved with someone.

What does it mean to be "ready" for a new intimate relationship? In a general sense, it means feeling psychologically and emotionally fit to begin a new, loving partnership. Since no one is without insecurities or faults, what can you look for as indicators of your readiness?

Being ready for a new intimate relationship implies that you honestly feel good about yourself. Do you truly believe you deserve a trusting, loving, respectful, abuse-free relationship? Are you confident that you can be a terrific partner for someone? In other words, is your self-esteem strong enough for you to enter a relationship as an *equal* partner? This sense of yourself as someone who had a fundamental right to equality in a relationship is necessary for the success of any future healthy relationship.

Another indicator of your readiness for a new relationship involves how well you have dealt with the difficult issues in your life following the abuse, such as depression, fear, difficulty in trusting others, anger, and problems with alcohol or other drugs. Although the thought of having someone in your life to support and love you may be very tempting, you want to be sure that you can offer your partner the love and caring you know you are capable of giving. After what you've been through, it would be unfair to yourself to begin a new relationship angry, depressed, or addicted. These will only cause you to feel bad about yourself and unworthy of your partner. If there is a possibility of a new intimate partner in your life, you both should be willing to take it slowly and wait until you feel that you are whole again and truly ready for the give-and-take a successful relationship requires.

New relationships can be exciting and exhilarating, but they can also be stressful. Any life change, good or bad, brings with it some degree of stress. Before you begin a new partnership, be sure that the other sources of stress in your life, or most of them at least, are manageable. The last thing you want is to start a new relationship feeling totally overwhelmed by other issues. All good relationships take time, energy, and work.

If your former partner sexually assaulted you, you may need to work through some of that trauma before being intimate with a new partner. You may have been able to do this on your own, or it may need the assistance of a professional counselor. Either way, when you become intimate with your next partner, the prospect of the experience and the experience itself should be loving and pleasurable for you. It should not cause you to feel afraid, ashamed, or overwhelmed.

Beginning a new relationship can be a frightening venture given the trauma you have experienced. Don't allow someone to talk you into something before you are ready. When the time is right, you will be able to stand your ground and take the time you need to explore a new partner and establish a new, healthy relationship.

A New Relationship, a New Beginning

At some point, you will begin to look forward to a new, healthy intimate relationship. At the same time you may continue to feel some very real fear about taking that risk. There are countless valid reasons for your fear and hesitation. Probably, what you fear more than anything else is the chance you will become involved with another abusive man. Although that fear is perfectly normal, if you approach new relationships with caution, and the wisdom that comes from experience, your fear will give way to a healthy connection with a loving partner. This will not happen overnight, but it will come with time.

What to Look For and What to Avoid

The ease with which you are able to complete this exercise may offer you some clues about your readiness for a new relationship.

1. List five qualities you will absolutely require in a new partner. These are nonnegotiable.

   QUALITIES I WILL REQUIRE:

   1. _____

   2. _____

   3. _____

   4. _____

   5. _____

2. List five qualities you will positively avoid in a new partner. These are unacceptable.

   QUALITIES I WILL NOT ACCEPT:

   1. _____

   2. _____

   3. _____

   4. _____

   5. _____

Postscript

The transition from an abusive or violent relationship to your new, confident, safe, and abuse-free life is an exciting yet difficult journey. You are re-creating your true self as you grow and move beyond your insecurities, confusion, self-doubts, fear, and dread. You are, in a most basic sense, transporting yourself from a kind of terrible darkness into the dawn of hope and optimism. This is just the beginning of a journey. You are working on yourself and your life. You are changing.

If you have any doubt about your desire and ability to make positive and healthy changes in yourself and your life, the evidence is right in front of you. You have read this book. That, by itself, is a positive sign of your desire to overcome your past. You may have a long way to go to reach the life you envision, or you may be almost there, but if you did not care, if you were not motivated to achieve your goals, you would not have bothered with the information and guidance this book has to offer.

We are not saying it will always be easy. Changing your life and emerging from the horrors of abuse are difficult transitions. However, we truly believe, in our hearts and in our minds, that survivors of relationship abuse and domestic violence have within them the strength, will, and personal power to transform their lives, to be loved and respected by others, to establish healthy, caring relationships, and to be *happy*.

We wish you an inspiring, wondrous, and successful journey.

Meg Dugan
Roger Hock

Resources

The following resources are included to help you read more about relationship abuse and domestic violence and to assist you in obtaining the support you need in your ongoing process of healing.

BOOKS

Relationship Abuse and Domestic Violence

Enns, G., & Black, J. (1997). *It's not okay anymore: Your personal guide to ending abuse, taking charge and loving yourself.* Oakland, CA: New Harbinger.

Evans, P. (1992). *Verbal abuse survivors speak out.* Holbrook, MA: Bob Adams.

Herman, J. L. (1992). *Trauma and recovery.* New York: Basic Books.

Matsakis, A. (1998). *Trust after trauma: A guide to relationships for survivors and those who love them.* Oakland, CA: New Harbinger.

NiCarthy, G. (1997). *Getting free: You can end abuse and take back your life.* Seattle, WA: Seal Press.

Statman, J. B. (1995). *The battered woman's survival guide: Breaking the cycle.* Dallas, TX: Taylor.

Abuse and Spirituality

Brady, A. D. (1994). *I survived: True encounters of a battered woman.* Landover, MD: Adrianne D. Brady.

Brady, A. D. (1997). *Life after abuse: Survivor of domestic violence.* Landover, MD: Adrianne D. Brady.

Alcohol & Other Drug Concerns

Fanning, P., & O'Neill, J. (1996). *The addictions workbook: A step-by-step guide to quitting alcohol and drugs.* Oakland, CA: New Harbinger.

Trimpey, J. (1996). *Rational recovery: The new cure for substance addiction.* New York: Pocket Books.

Anger Management and Depression

Copeland, M. E., & McKay, M. (1992). *The depression workbook: A guide for living with depression and manic depression.* Oakland, CA: New Harbinger.

Potter-Efron, R., & Potter-Efron, R. T. (1994). *Angry all the time: An emergency guide to anger control.* Oakland, CA: New Harbinger.

Weisinger, H. (1985). *Dr. Weisinger's anger work-out book.* New York: William Morrow.

Yapko, M. D. (1998). *Breaking the patterns of depression.* New York: Main Street Books.

Anxiety and Stress

Alman, B. M., & Lambrou, P. (1992). *Self-hypnosis: The complete manual for health and self-change.* New York: Brunner/Mazel.

Bernard, L. C., & Krupat, E. (1994). *Health psychology: Biophysical factors in health and illness.* Fort Worth, TX: Harcourt Brace.

Bourne, E. J. (1995). *The anxiety and phobia workbook.* Oakland, CA: New Harbinger.

Davis, M. (1995). *The relaxation and stress reduction workbook.* Oakland, CA: New Harbinger.

Gawain, S. (1983). *Creative visualizations.* San Rafael, CA: New World Library.

Gawain, S. (1995). *The creative visualization workbook.* San Rafael, CA: New World Library.

Peurifoy, R. Z. (1995). *Anxiety, phobias, and panic: A step-by-step program for regaining control of your life.* New York: Warner Books.

Smith, H. (1994). *The 10 natural laws of successful time and life management.* New York: Warner Books.

Children

Fassler, D., & Dumas, L. (1998). *Help me, I'm sad: Recognizing, treating, and preventing childhood depression.* New York: Viking.

Ingersoll, B., & Goldstein, S. (1996). *Lonely, sad and angry: A parent's guide to depression in children and adolescents.* New York: Main Street Books.

Johnson, J., & O'Neill, C. (1999). *How do I feel about being angry?* New York: Copper Beech Books.

March, J. (1995). *Anxiety disorders in children and adolescents.* New York: Guilford Press.

Shaw, M. (1995). *Your anxious child: Raising a healthy child in a frightening world.* New York: Birch Lane Press.

Smith, M., & Berry, B. (1996). *Let's talk about feeling angry.* New York: Scholastic Trade.

Loss

Bullitt, D. (1996). *Filling the void: Six steps from loss to fulfillment.* New York: Scribner.

Coryell, D. (1997). *Good grief: Healing through the shadow of loss.* Santa Fe, NM: The Shiva Foundation.

Doak, D. (1996). *Coming to life: A companion piece to the self-exploration process.* Nevada City, CA: Blue Dolphin.

Goldman, L. (1996). *Breaking the silence: A guide to help children with complicated grief: Suicide, homicide, AIDS, violence, and abuse.* Philadelphia: Accelerated Development.

James, J., & Friedman, R. (1998). *The grief recovery handbook: The action program for moving beyond death, divorce, and other losses.* New York: HarperCollins.

Koman, A. (1998). *How to mend a broken heart: Letting go and moving on.* Chicago: NTC/Contemporary Publishing.

Metrick, S. (1994). *Crossing the bridge: Creating ceremonies for grieving and healing from life's losses.* Berkeley, CA: Celestial Arts.

Self-Esteem

English, M. (1992). *How to feel great about yourself and your life.* New York: Amacon.

Field, L. (1993). *Creating self-esteem.* Shaftesbury, Dorset, Rockport, MA, and Brisbane, Queensland: Element.

McKay, M., & Fanning, P. (1993). *Self-esteem.* Oakland, CA. New Harbinger.

Sorensen, M. J. (1998). *Breaking the chain of low self-esteem.* Sherwood, OR: Wolf.

Self-Harm

Smith, G., Cox, D., & Saradjian, J. (1998). *Women and self-harm: Understanding, coping, and healing from self-mutilation*. New York. Routledge.

Sexual Assault

Benedict, H., & Brison, S. (1994). *Recovery: How to survive sexual assault for women, men, teenagers, and their families*. New York. Columbia University Press.

Fay, J., & Adams, C. (1990). *Free of the shadows: Recovering from sexual violence*. Oakland, CA: New Harbinger.

Finney, L. D. (1992). *Reach for the Rainbow: Advanced healing for survivors of sexual assault*. New York. Perigee.

Maltz, W., & Arian, C. (1992). *The sexual healing journey: A guide for survivors of sexual abuse*. New York. HarperPerennial Library.

INTERNET RESOURCES

Citizens Opposed to Domestic Violence
1-800-868-CODA (2632)
http://bftpolice.com/coda/p0000114.html

"Domestic Violence.com"
http://www.dvguide.com/

Domestic Violence Resources on the WWW
http://www.geocities.com/Wellesley/2266/dv.html

The Family Violence Prevention Fund
http://www.fvpf.org

Feminist Majority's Domestic Violence Information Center
http://www.feminist.org/911/crisis.html

National Domestic Violence Hotline, Department of Justice, Violence Against Women Office
1-800-799-SAFE (7233) or 1-800-787-3224 (TDD)
http://www.usdoj.gov/vawo/

Index